Midquest

Other books by Fred Chappell

The World Between the Eyes

It Is Time, Lord

The Inkling

Dagon

The Gaudy Place

Moments of Light

Awakening to Music

LOUISIANA STATE UNIVERSITY PRESS

Midquest A Poem

Fred Chappell

BATON ROUGE AND LONDON 1981

Manufactured in the United States of America

Design: Albert Crochet
Typeface: VIP Garamond

Louisiana Paperback Edition, 1989
98 97 96 95 94 93 92 91 90 89   5 4 3 2 1

LIBRARY OF CONGRESS CATALOGING IN PUBLICATION DATA

Chappell, Fred, 1936–
    Midquest: a poem.

    I. Title.
PS3553.H298M5   811'.54   81-8474

ISBN 0-8071-0877-4 (cloth)
ISBN 0-8071-1580-0 (paper)

Contents

Preface

The four volumes *River, Bloodfire, Wind Mountain,* and *Earthsleep* comprise the single long poem *Midquest.* It is an odd sort of performance, something like a verse novel, each of the four parts focused upon one of the classical four elements, each book made up of eleven longish poems and together covering four times the same twenty-four hours of the speaker's life. These twenty-four hours occur on his thirty-fifth birthday, but not every hour here is in present time; many hours are given to reminiscence of the same hour at an earlier period of his life. (Breakfast, for example, is not drawn in present time, but the speaker remembers a breakfast with his father seventeen years earlier in a hunting cabin.) Numbers, then, are obviously important in the poem. Dante chose his thirty-fifth birthday to take stock of himself; four is the Pythagorean number representing World, and $4 \times 11 = 44$, the world twice, interior and exterior. Etc., etc.

A wide variety of verse forms are called on for these 44. Free verse and blank verse predominate, are the basic "stitches," representing different states of mind, but we have also terza rima, Yeatsian tetrameter, rhymed couplets, syllabics, classical hexameter variation, elegiacs, chant royal, and so forth. The structural forms too are various, with dramatic monologue, interior monologue, epistle, a playet, elegy, and other sorts. With this variety of forms I hoped to suggest a kind of melting pot American quality, and in fact my model was that elder American art form, the sampler, each form standing for a different fancy stitch.

And each of the volumes (except *Wind Mountain*) is organized as a balancing act. The first poem is mirrored by the last; the second by the next to last, and so on inward. But the sixth poem in each volume is companionless in that volume, and concerned with a garrulous old gentleman named Virgil Campbell, who is supposed to give to the whole its specifically regional, its Appalachian, context. The fifth poem in each is given to stream of consciousness and these interior monologues become discernibly more formal as the speaker begins to order his life. Each volume is dominated by a different element of the family, *River* by the grandparents, *Bloodfire* by the father, and there is a family reunion in *Earthsleep,* the part most shadowed by death. (In order to suggest the fluid and disordered nature of air, *Wind Mountain* was exempt from some of these requirements.)

There are many minor motivic points of organization. The mother always speaks, or tries to speak, of the difficulties of mountain living and for leitmotif is given the word *hard.* The grandmother thinks always of the family and becomes aggrieved at its dissolution under force of time. A burned-down church is importantly not there from *River* on. The first line of *Earthsleep* completes the sentence for the last line of *Wind Mountain.* The first poem in each volume is an overture, intimating all the themes of the whole, but emphasizing the dominant element in the volume at hand. Etc., etc., etc., etc.

Though he is called "Fred," the "I" of the poem is no more myself than any character in any novel I might choose to write. (And no less myself, either, I suppose.) He was constructed, as was Dante's persona, Dante, in order to be widely representative. He was reared on a farm but has moved to the city; he has deserted manual for intellectual labor, is "upwardly mobile"; he is cut off from his disappearing cultural traditions but finds them, in remembering, his real values. He is to some extent a demographic sample.

Ours is the time of the brilliant autobiographical lyric. Many of the fine qualities of this sort of poem—intensity, urgency, metaphysical trial, emotional revelation—are absent from *Midquest.* I wished to capture, to restore to my work other qualities sometimes lacking in the larger body of contemporary poetry: detachment, social scope, humor, portrayal of character and background, discursiveness, wide range of subject matter. So that *Midquest* is to some degree a reactionary work.

The poems in the forefront of my mind during composition, the poets I felt a respectfully distant kinship with, are old ones indeed. Dante, first of all, because of design; and then Chaucer, Dryden, Browning, Horace, John Gay, Byron, Boileau, Hebbel. Some fiction writers stayed on the edge of my mind, Chekhov and Mann as always, but also Sarah Orne Jewett and Mary Wilkins Freeman. Some of the grand idols of my admiration—Baudelaire, Rimbaud, Rilke, Pound—did not show up, or appeared only in order to be made fun of.

But *Midquest* is reactionary for a purpose. A contemporary poet would be mad to turn his back upon contemporary idiom and upon post-Symbolist advances in sensibility if he had not some different and well-defined goal. For purposes of design, it seemed to me I had to choose, and so I grasped about in the past for conformable examples. The question then becomes whether I lost more than I gained, a question not fitting nor indeed possible for me to answer.

Old Fred is not much disposed to applaud himself for this or any other performance; apology and even recrimination are his deeper talents. But he does hope that a reader may find *Midquest* accessible and amusing even in its imperfections, and that some solace may be taken from it. For it is, after all, in its largest design a love poem.

River

Let the most absent-minded of men be plunged in his deepest reveries—stand that man on his legs, set his feet a-going, and he will infallibly lead you to water, if water there be in all that region. Should you ever be athirst in the great American desert, try this experiment, if your caravan happen to be supplied with a metaphysical professor. Yes, as every one knows, meditation and water are wedded for ever.

—Moby-Dick

I   The River Awakening in the Sea

Deep morning. Before the trees take silhouettes.

My forehead suckles your shoulder, straining to hear
In you the headlong ocean, your blood, island-saying sea now.
Wild stretches, bound to every water, of seas in you,
Uttering foam islands like broad flotillas of cabbage butterflies.
Gray tall clouds vaguely scribbling the pages of sea-top.
Your small breathing gently whetted in your nostrils, suffusing
The blood-warm pillowslip. Bedroom curls and uncurls with breath.
And all houses dark and nothing astir, though no one
Is truly asleep, everyone begins slowly to reach toward another,
Entering to each other with hands and arms impalpable, shadowless.
Slowly they turn dreaming as waves above roll deeper waves beneath.
Now they murmur amorphous words,
Words far away, no more guessable than the currents
Beginning to shudder and tremble as the hour enlarges.
Strands of current nudge into arpeggios the wide keyboards of whitebait.

                                 Perhaps now in you my body
Seeks limits, now contoured horizons
Deliver to self accustomed bitter edges.
Deliver to the man, plunging narrow in the sea, curb and margin.

Or wind diving out of the sky and raising
In the waters falling towers of lace and spittle,
Oaring underneath with strong legs so tides pile and gasp.
So corded surf comes forward half-circle,
Spreading and cataracting.

                                 We are fitful in the sheets,
We clutch. My forearm digging your breast,
I am swimming your salt skin.
Early light, stringent, has opened the bedroom, searches

Crease between wall and ceiling and molds itself on the dresser
In domestic shapes: brush and comb, deodorant can, cologne bottles,
Black clots of hairpins like barbwire.
Torn sheet of light sizzles in the mirror.

Sea coming apart now, green fingers
Shaking and shredding like cobweb. The sky
Punishes the waves, in-thrusts glassy caves,
Caves growing mouthlike round spindles of wind.

Do you dream of falling?
I dream your mouth gasps numbly open, your breath caught back pulsing,
Arms outflung, protesting reckless deeps you do not escape.

How the world was formed,
The dead dropped down brick by brick to sea bottom,
The dead and the sleeping, layer upon
Layer, they hug each other forever, their bones
Grin in the fathomless dark, wary as eyes.
Here is the bedrock: the dead, fold upon fold.
Lamprotoxu, Chiasmodon,
Dragonfish, Sea Viper, Black Gulper,
Burning like comets over choked bones.

While I am wishing never to wake, the oily bull-muscle
Of sea water shoves us landward, straining and warping like kites.
Yellow ring of earth rises above burned eyes.
My senses touch daylight and recoil, the furious net
Of daylight plumbs the bed.

Continent or momentary island,
Mid-life, this land too known, too much unknown, 28 May 1971,
First day of my thirty-fifth year.
Sleeping sleeping I cannot halt the faithless instinct to be born.

The trees glow with raucous birds.
I rise and yawn,
Begin to scratch for clothing.

My naked foot upon this alien floor.

2

II   Birthday 35: Diary Entry

1.

Multiplying my age by 2 in my head,
I'm a grandfather. Or dead.

"Midway in this life I came to a darksome wood."
But Dante, however befuddled, was Good.

And to be Good, in any viable sense,
Demands the wrought-iron primness of a Georgetown fence.

I'm still in flight, still unsteadily in pursuit,
Always becoming more sordid, pale, and acute . . .

For all the good it does . . . I'd rather seize by the neck
Some Golden Opportunity and with a mastiff shake

Empty its pockets of change;
And let my life grow bearded and strange.

In Mexico, Hunza, or Los Angeles,
I'd smoke a ton of dope and minister my fleas.

Or retiring to Monument Valley alone
With Gauguin, I'd take up saxophone.

Or slipping outside time to a Heavenly Escurial,
I'd spend a thousand years at a Monogram serial.

For though I've come so far that nothing intriguing will happen,
Like every half-assed politico I keep my options open.

My style's to veer and slide and wobble,
Immorally eavesdropping my own Babel.

When Plato divided us into Doers and Thinkers,
He didn't mean corporate generals and autoerotic bankers;

He meant that one attunes his nerves to Mind,
Or is blind.

Will may go stupid; clumsy its dance,
Mired in marmalade of circumstance.

Abjure, therefore, no ounce of alcohol.
Keep desultory and cynical.

On paper I scribble mottoes and epigrams,
Blessings and epithets, O-Holy's and Damn's—

Not matter sufficient to guard a week by.
The wisdom I hoard you could stuff in your eye.

But *everything* means *something,* that's my faith;
Despair begins when they stop my mouth.

Drunk as St. Francis I preach to the cat.
I even talk back to the TV set.

Sometimes I even Inquisition my wife:
"Susan, *is* there a moral alternative to life?"

Partly because I want to know, partly because
I'm amused by sleazy cleverness.

I can talk till the moon dissolves, till the stars
Splash down in the filth of morning newspapers.

Talk that engenders a fearful itch
Always just barely not quite out of reach.

Talk with purposes so huge and vague,
The minor details are Om and Egg.

Surely something gets said if only in intent,
When the magnesium candle of enthusiasm is burnt.

Happy Birthday to me! At age thirty-five
I scratch to see if I'm yet alive.

Thumbing the ledger of thirty-five years,
I find unstartled I'm badly in arrears.

In fact, I'm up to my eyes in debt
Unpayable. And not done suffering yet.

But then, so what?
What you think you owe is everything you're not.

That's not true debt, but merely guilt,
Irrelevant though heartfelt;

Merely part of the noisy lovers' quarrel
We name Doctrine, Dialectic, and Moral.

I'd sleep in the eiderdown of the True Believer
And never nightmare about Either/Or

If I had a different person in my head.
But this gnawing worm shows that I'm not dead.

Therefore: either I live with doubt
Or get out.

2.

(While I ponder and point this offhand apologia
for a life I find ungainly and sinister as
a black umbrella, my gaze settles and unsettles
in the bourgeois landscape outside the window where:
a row of day lilies gives a livid razzberry to
the beige terrier peeing against our dented
garbage can with all the complacent unconcern
of a Polish steelworker who once went four
bloody rounds with Carmen Basilio and by
God doesn't care who knows it.
                                        If I
could choose I'd be the sunlight which comes
down like melting butter, dripping in white
spots the flanks of things and carbonating the

5

dog's not-quite-tan stiff hairs one by one.
That is a mode of being, just but not
fatuous, which one aches for but cannot
—without madness—strive toward, alas.

Do dogs keep diaries? Do lilies?

They should.)

3.

I'd like to believe anything is possible.
That I could walk out on a midnight full

Of stars and hear an omniscient Voice say,
"Well, Fred, for a change you had a good day.

You didn't do anything so terribly awful.
Even your thoughts were mostly lawful.

I'm pleased." —Or that by accident I'd find
A tablet headed, *Carry this message to mankind.*

—Or that simply by dreaming I'd find out
What subnuclear physics is all about.

But nothing like that is in the cards.
Bit by scroungy bit knowledge affords

Itself; and what the angels know, or don't,
My brain would reduce absolutely to cant.

Wherefore, my soul, be thou content.
"Man, I'd love to, but I *ain't.*"

Why not? Each time I reach outside my skin,
I just get lonesome for what's within.

I know the future I will not trust,
And here in the present as an overnight guest

At the Holiday Inn of Crooked Dream
I nurse the one-eyed flame

Of bitter regret
And shriek "You bastards haven't got me yet!"

At phantoms who know damn well they have,
Now and to the hour of the grave.

Whatever they say, Time's not a river;
It is a slow harsh fever

Of things trying not to go smash,
A wilderness of wind and ash.

When I went to the river I saw willows
Splashing down, oil-slick of pinks and yellows

And purples, and leaning over the edge of grass
I saw, darkened, my own face.

On the bank of Time I saw nothing human,
No man, no woman,

No animals or plants; only moon
Upon moon, sterile stone

Climbing the steep hill of void.
And I was afraid.

Please, Lord. I want to go to some forever
Where water is, and live there.

I want a sky that rain drops from,
Soothing the intemperate loam;

An eternity where a man can buy a drink
For a buddy, or a good-looking chick.

If there's no hereafter with hot and cold running
I'm simply not coming.

Not that I doubt Your willingness to provide,
But, Lord, You stand on one side

Of the infinite black ditch
And I on the other. *And that's a bitch.*

But I'm going to take it for granted
That honey Elysium is plentifully planted

With trout streams and waterfalls and suburban
Swimming pools, and sufficient chaser for bourbon.

Lead me then, Lord, to the thundering valleys where
Cool silver droplets feather the air;

Where rain like thimbles smacks roofs of tin,
Washing away sin;

Where daily a vast and wholesome cloud
Announces itself aloud.

Amen.

III My Grandmother Washes Her Feet

I see her still, unsteadily riding the edge
Of the clawfoot tub, mumbling to her feet,
Musing bloodrust water about her ankles.
Cotton skirt pulled up, displaying bony
Bruised patchy calves that would make you weep.

Rinds of her soles had darkened, crust-colored—
Not yellow now—like the tough outer belly
Of an adder. In fourteen hours the most refreshment
She'd given herself was dabbling her feet in the water.

"You mightn't've liked John-Giles. Everybody knew
He was a mean one, galloping whiskey and bad women
All night. Tried to testify dead drunk
In church one time. That was a ruckus. Later
Came back a War Hero, and all the young men
Took to doing the things he did. And failed.
Finally one of his women's men shot him."

"What for?"

                    "Stealing milk through fences . . . . That part
Of Family nobody wants to speak of.
They'd rather talk about fine men, brick houses,
Money. Maybe you ought to know, teach you
Something."

                    "What *do* they talk about?"

                                        "Generals,
And the damn Civil War, and marriages.
Things you brag about in the front of Bibles.

You'd think there was arms and legs of Family
On every battlefield from Chickamauga
To Atlanta."

        "That's not the way it is?"

"Don't matter how it is. No proper way
To talk, is all. It was nothing they ever did.
And plenty they *won't* talk about . . . John-Giles!"

Her cracked toes thumped the tub wall, spreading
Shocklets. Amber toenails curled like shavings.
She twisted the worn knob to pour in coolness
I felt suffuse her body like a whiskey.

"Bubba Martin, he was another, and no
Kind of man. Jackleg preacher with the brains
Of a toad. Read the Bible upsidedown and crazy
Till it drove him crazy, making crazy marks
On doorsills, windows, sides of Luther's barn.
He killed hisself at last with a shotgun.
No gratitude for Luther putting him up
All those years. Shot so he'd fall down the well."

"I never heard."

        "They never mention him.
Nor Aunt Annie, that everybody called
Paregoric Annie, that roamed the highways
Thumbing cars and begging change to keep
Even with her craving. She claimed she was saving up
To buy a glass eye. It finally shamed them
Enough, they went together and got her one.
That didn't stop her. She lugged it around
In a velvet-lined case, asking strangers
Please to drop it in the socket for her.
They had her put away. And that was that.
There's places Family ties just won't stretch to."

Born then in my mind a race of beings
Unknown and monstrous. I named them Shadow-Cousins,
A linked long dark line of them,
Peering from mirrors and gleaming in closets, agog
To manifest themselves inside myself.
Like discovering a father's cancer.
I wanted to search my body for telltale streaks.

"Sounds like a bunch of cow thieves."

                                            "Those too, I reckon,
But they're forgotten or covered over so well
Not even I can make them out. Gets foggy
When folks decide they're coming on respectable.
First thing you know, you'll have a Family Tree."

(I imagined a wind-stunted horse-apple.)

She raised her face. The moons of the naked bulb
Flared in her spectacles, painting out her eyes.
In dirty water light bobbed like round soap.
A countenance matter-of-fact, age-engraved,
Mulling in peaceful wonder petty annals
Of embarrassment. Gray but edged with brown
Like an old photograph, her hair shone yellow.
A tiredness mantled her fine energy.
She shifted, sluicing water under instep.

"O what's the use," she said. "Water seeks
Its level. If your daddy thinks that teaching school
In a white shirt makes him a likelier man,
What's to blame? Leastways, he won't smother
Of mule-farts or have to starve for a pinch of rainfall.
Nothing new gets started without the old's
Plowed under, or halfway under. We sprouted from dirt,
Though, and it's with you, and dirt you'll never forget."

"No Mam."

"Don't you say me No Mam yet.
Wait till you get your chance to deny it."

Once she giggled, a sound like stroking muslin.

"You're bookish. I can see you easy a lawyer
Or a county clerk in a big white suit and tie,
Feeding the preacher and bribing the sheriff and the judge.
Second-generation-respectable
Don't come to any better destiny.
But it's dirt you rose from, dirt you'll bury in.
Just about the time you'll think your blood
Is clean, here will come dirt in a natural shape
You never dreamed. It'll rise up saying, Fred,
Where's that mule you're supposed to march behind?
Where's your overalls and roll-your-owns?
Where's your Blue Tick hounds and Domineckers?
Not all the money in this world can wash true-poor
True rich. Fatback just won't change to artichokes."

"What's artichokes?"

                              "Pray Jesus you'll never know.
For if you do it'll be a sign you've grown
Away from what you are, can fly to flinders
Like a touch-me-not . . . I may have errored
When I said *true-poor*. It ain't the same
As dirt-poor. When you got true dirt you got
Everything you need . . . And don't you say me
Yes Mam again. You just wait."

                              She leaned
And pulled the plug. The water circled gagging
To a bloody eye and poured in the hole like a rat.
I thought maybe their spirits had gathered there,
All my Shadow-Cousins clouding the water,
And now they ran to earth and would cloud the earth.
Effigies of soil, I could seek them out

By clasping soil, forcing warm rude fingers
Into ancestral jelly my father wouldn't plow.
I strained to follow them, and never did.
I never had the grit to stir those guts.
I never had the guts to stir that earth.

IV   Cleaning the Well

Two worlds there are. One you think
You know; the Other is the Well.
In hard December down I went.
"Now clean it out good." Lord, I sank
Like an anchor. My grand-dad leant
Above. His face blazed bright as steel.

Two worlds, I tell you. Swallowed by stones
Adrip with sweat, I spun on the ache
Of the rope; the pulley shrieked like bones
Scraped merciless on violins.
Plunging an eye. Plunging a lake
Of corkscrew vertigo and silence.

I halfway knew the rope would break.

Two suns I entered. At exact noon
The white sun narrowly hung above;
Below, like an acid floating moon,
The sun of water shone.
And what beneath that? A monster trove

Of blinding treasure I imagined:
Ribcage of drowned warlock gleaming,
Rust-chewed chain mail, or a plangent
Sunken bell tolling to the heart
Of earth. (They'd surely chosen an art-
less child to sound this soundless dreaming

O.) Dropping like a meteor,
I cried aloud—"Whoo! It's *God
Damn* cold!"—dancing the skin of the star.

"You watch your mouth, young man," he said.
I jerked and cursed in a silver fire
Of cold. My left leg thrummed like a wire.

Then, numb. Well water rose to my waist
And I became a figure of glass,
A naked explorer of outer space.
Felt I'd fricasseed my ass.
Felt I could stalk through earth and stone,
Nerveless creature without a bone.

Water-sun shattered, jelly-
bright wavelets lapped the walls.
Whatever was here to find, I stood
In the lonesome icy belly
Of the darkest vowel, lacking breath and balls,
Brain gummed mud.

"Say, Fred, how's it going down there?"
His words like gunshots roared; re-roared.
I answered, "Well—" (*Well well well* . . .)
And gave it up. It goes like Hell,
I thought. Precise accord
Of pain, disgust, and fear.

"Clean it out good." He drifted pan
And dipper down. I knelt and dredged
The well floor. Ice-razors edged
My eyes, the blackness flamed like fever,
Tin became nerve in my hand
Bodiless. *I shall arise never.*

What did I find under this black sun?
Twelve plastic pearls, monopoly
Money, a greenish rotten cat,
Rubber knife, toy gun,

Clock guts, wish book, door key,
An indescribable female hat.

Was it worth the trip, was it true Descent?
Plumbing my childhood, to fall
Through the hole in the world and become . . .
What? *He told me to go. I went.*
(Recalling something beyond recall.
Cold cock on the nether roof of Home.)

Slouch sun swayed like a drunk
As up he hauled me, up, up,
Most willing fish that was ever caught.
I quivered galvanic in the taut
Loop, wobbled on the solid lip
Of earth, scarcely believing my luck.

His ordinary world too rich
For me, too sudden. Frozen blue,
Dead to armpit, I could not keep
My feet. I shut my eyes to fetch
Back holy dark. Now I knew
All my life uneasy sleep.

Jonah, Joseph, Lazarus,
Were you delivered so? Ript untimely
From black wellspring of death, unseemly
Haste of flesh dragged forth?
Artemis of waters, succor us,
Oversurfeit with our earth.

My vision of light trembled like steam.
I could not think. My senses drowned
In Arctic Ocean, the Pleiades
Streaked in my head like silver fleas.
I could not say what I had found.
I cannot say my dream.

When life began re-tickling my skin
My bones shuddered me. Sun now stood
At one o'clock. Yellow. Thin.
I had not found death good.
"Down there I kept thinking I was dead."

"Aw, you're all right," he said.

V   Susan Bathing

> Here Earth and Water seem to strive again,
> Not *Chaos*-like together crush'd and bruis'd,
> But as the World, harmoniously confus'd.
>
> —Alexander Pope
> *Windsor Forest*

You
are rejoicement, fair flesh erect in the porcelain & the
bee-eyed steel showerhead ogling & touching you and
I would make a Renaissance poet's wish, to be the pleasing
showerhead touching you with a hundred streaming fingers
wandering so close your body completely to your feet, or
I wish to be the worn white tub you stand in, would
be like a snowy garden with a single grand delicate flower
or a fountain which receives or maybe a statue which was never
shaped nor even dreamed of but nevertheless was born in and from
earth of antiquity, exhumed time past standing wet to haunt time
present & to encroach now upon sleeping and waking, every moment
to darken and illumine at once like the picnic ground in the oak
grove when June wind sifts like a dropped poker
deck the deep green leaves above, fluttery tide of them untying
itself upon a breaker of breeze, and you & I beneath swing between
us the wicker basket & wool army blanket, coming to the shade wary
for acrid horsenettle and dried buggy cowflop, because this is how I
pray we shall together die, coming forward to the shade hand in hand,
alert & neither happy nor grieving & our spirits together as close as
at this moment upon your flushed skin the soapy warm hand of water is
spread and slides, for a second pausing about your feet & then drifting
to the dark naught of the drain and going away, just as many times
in dreams I have sweated to chase some quick gleam of you instantly
unrecognized & then too eagerly leaped at, & then it darted gone
forever through a silent hole in my mind like childhood dragon

flies I pursued iridescent in sunlight & precious but in the shadow under
Beaverdam Creek Bridge invisible, uncatchable, becoming creatures only
of remorseful imagination, but these dreamed partial ghosts now obliterate
as now I see all your naked animal moving under drumming
water, strong neck grown taut & misty droplets smudge your chin
and as you scrub the azure cloth on your left shoulder the right elbow
thrusts out of plane, obtruding the perfect distance between us & therefore
has made claim, living and tactile and feeling, upon my own space of
breathing & feeling, upon my responsibilities to whatever is genuine, for you
are I know actual, actual and urgent as starvation and all other
rational disasters & botches of mortality, more actual
than these because your reddened elbow pokes forward into time
present iterating that beauty too is Jesus! urgent (*O what shall
I do with my hands & paunch? shall I hide my eyes? my face
in my hands blots to a mush like a rotten canteloupe*), that
unattending beauty is danger & mortal sin, and that no matter how my
heart is abashed & my senses quaked in the viscera, I
must cleave to speech, speech being my single knowledge, speech-praise,
though this speech clings only a soiled atomic
instant about your bare feet before pouring fast to the black
mouth of the pipe to smother in dirt and stone, yet why
should you not accept my words as water for water also would
be praise freely burgeoning out of air and friendly upon the skin
to gladden nerve-ends so the pores shall open & sing unsounding
like baby swallows when the mother darts quick out of open
air, ordinary as a summer shower, bringing lunch, this if only
once I could know surely you opened to praise, unfolded unthinking
like a cold hand brought to the campfire, and why not *why not*
saying of praise as instrument of unclosing and rising toward light
& free water, for if not praiseful speech the spirit is stopped off
in the throat where the clavicles come near to join before the body
begins to fever & tremble frustrate like a grenade which was aching
& aching to devour itself in a fountain of light & surprise, and
do not halt it, for once the mind prepares to praise & garbs
in worshipful robe it enlarges to plenitude, vastness of names

qualities numbers and points of kinship, and a criminal cheap
death ensues if it cannot utter, as my mouth utters water having
now become the stainless showerhead to search you with a hundred
tongues, slope and shadow of you, hollow of your shoulder where
dim soapfleece lingers & the eyelid-shaped shadows beneath your
breasts & strands of shining bone at wrists silvery as trout bellies
& loose fingerlings of hair damp-curling beside the ear & on your
pink flanks water a moment holding in little beads like dew on
the bedroom window with new sun behind & shining through as your skin
in this water flames & small of your back gently curving so the drops
collect in a transparent pendant delta & the crisp fleece before sequined
and thrilling with drops like a G-string in white bare light turned
on after all the sailors are hauled away drunk rubbing palms across
bleeding lips, & in this spangled fleece is a singular water also
praise, speech-praise spoken from necessity & to keep alive praise
in the sweet creatures in their cores & the smooth thighs veiny
with water errant and trackless though discoverable always discoverable
in clarity, thigh slightly shuddering at the cool accidental touch
of wall tile & then toward my mouth saying all this in water you raise
& open your mouth and I enter in & am warm in tongue and throat until
through praise I begin to suffuse all through you and even to emerge
all about you a radiance shining like silver leaf smeared around a
pensive joyous Tuscan madonna seeing Latin tumble backward out of
the annunciation angel's mouth and who has not quite opened yet her
mouth to receive the news pouring forward, news which also is praise
of woman, Ave, plena gratia, Woman thou shalt with thy flesh utter
living one word origin and end of praise forever, praise to suffer
violate inviolable amid black shame and stony unknowing of those
who grudge hate maim & murder & finally deafen themselves to even
the great waters all day and night traversing the heavens & under whose
shadows they harm & kill, ignorant that shade of water is light, that death
shall be method of praise under a sky which rains the light &
water mingled together from which our unenviable brotherhood arose, light
and water cleaving together as this too-cool bathroom light mixes drily
burning with each water-bead to form now you, Susan, as you that clean

space hold & compose as at once you burst it, jamming the whole
a thoughtful palpable object upon my flickering senses so that an
object impersonal also intimate as a touch at groin you are, as if
Clementia on heavy vellum page caught fire & scorched the tracks from my
finger ends & the nails melted & sparse hairs on my forearms flared
up, as if at the foot of my bed at midnight appeared a Sphinx of timeless
water gazing upon' me with pity too huge to say, bewailing me because
no word is so expressive as water which in her being she articulates & I
senseless & too broken to know and cannot advance to praise, my
mouth unhinged swinging idiot slack like the door of a ruined barn the wind
molests & my eyes filmed over with thick oils of self-pride, my skin
anesthetized deadly, so that in darkest waters of sleeping I move
unyielding to water, stolid mud mountain water enfolds & does not
enlighten, stockstill in my thought as if God had never said *Let there*
be, scissoring the firmaments, & the Sphinx of water shapes now Herself
to a single tear reflecting my chest & face elongate, scared by salt vision
of self-ignorance, seeing myself in bitter water stretched out in death
white & wavering wraithlike in a mirror containing me but which I cannot
touch, but here a clarifying suspicion approaches, that the Sphinx is
yourself, Susan, then when you wring rinsing the azure cloth at your waist,
upper arms at your ribs, your form now retreat into flattened space
suggesting eternity, only faintly human at this moment, outline
human as in Byzantine mosaics, but an obscuring water stands between us,
pallid cloud of steam shrugging upward its shoulders & its pearl
torso swelling forward maybe in threat but certainly your solid volume
veiled, so I must plead, Why do you go away? where do you go? will you
again return from behind the spiritual mists & acquaint again
my senses? or are you for good ascended into ideal spaces & rely upon
my hurt memory to limn your shape my heart starves to join, do not
so scar my will I plead you, for my will is stricken and contort,
its own most effort has fouled & burst it & only intercession from
without can restore it, and so I see grateful at last the toilet cistern
begin to sweat, the panes of the narrow window run in streaks, the mirror
show patches of white room with angles clear & strait, and thank God your
body! too reappears pink-glowing and spread about it its own scent,

washed skin renewed like a grand delicate flower rebloomed, and your
face I see lilylike shining light as porcelain beneath water shining
light, eyes dark but accustomed to this white light and intelligent
of form in all spaces & modes whatsoever, AND adoration in the wet
air coalesces, I can & will believe that hymns are sung and cherubim
puffing out their cheeks like chipmunks strew the gray linoleum with
evanescent flowers that touch & melt, snowflakes of flowers unique
& instantly mortal returned to soil of water, ubiquitous surface
reaching from this closed air and clasping, painting each sleek plane
as masseurs rubbed down the lion-colored wrestlers with oil so
they would appear immune to grasp, so that entrance to the space
Ajax collected insured not at all hand should find his lithe & strong
limbs and hold, in this manner you are seen, gauzy curtains of steam
drop away and all ablush and damp, tea-rose dew-drowned, you stand
a moment pensive before lifting the dun rough terry towel & loosing it,
folds disclosing in silent slow movement like a film warped almost
to timelessness, your flesh more fleshly-seeming because the cloth
opposes it in texture, and with it begin to swaddle your body, tugging &
twisting in its snug cocoon, and how will you now this chrysalis
exit, all over rubbed warm & smiling at last as if you dreamed
this very second you were not here, your body remaining yet sailed
away on streams of atoms into the winds and is sweetening now zephyrs
by Bermuda & Mykonos or gustily invading the spicy Virgins, it would be true
since I could I do believe your spirit has power in air, the same
dominion strong over land & sea that wind & water cherish, unspotted freedom
intact proud fierce if it come to point but happy & clear by nature and
by nature selfless of its own character as the dropping rivulet on
Fires Creek Mountain that fed & fed the moss-painted stone we saw, stone
greenly avid for water it can never digest and which again relooped
below sliding rot-black log & snaking under mirk humus & stone jumble
till we had mostly fallen the steep trail and saw this water quiet
& widen to a stream hand-broad final, its destination sure
to Little Fires where dark laurels hang over & black gnats swarm
in big funnel shapes & the rainbows lie still at boiling pool heads &
gurgle among rocks makes above the stream an elegant baroque

fountain of sound varying shapely refreshing as canon for clavier,
for I know it would be your nature to drift into the serious currents
of earth & sky, to nudge until absorbed by root & tendril, assuage
compassionately amative hungers, and so wherever you are you are
here too rubbing your left shin rested on the toilet seat so deliberately
you might be polishing marble, half-hypnotized by the pleasurable
warm abrading, knowing perhaps a distance obtains although your hand
moves on your pale leg, a distance between them obtains and though
touching they shall never meet, distance obtaining as between mouth
& word mouth forms, speech praise, fire carried up in a cave missing
its roof yet brightness reaches from the mouth outwards and is
known by who cares to see & hear, lighting what wishes to be lit, thus
you polish yourself as Catullus with pumice eternally scraped
from his word the verdigris and this is after all, Lady, what you are,
a word, maybe like Woodstar the name of a hummingbird or maybe
from books a classy Latin name for a flower Ipomoea purpurea dark
pink Morning Glory with a burst black star at center, bell of this
trumpet holding in one drop of early water the sun burning yellow
and drowned in that globe, plenum of dew, and if we march to fields
to see the universe made bitsy in the flower we shall feel about us
water-presence water-immanence though the sky be blue scoured
silk, a clear day & no hint of rain & mists blown away, yet
we shall feel at the backs of our necks water unstoppable in
arteries of grass vines and even the mica-flecked gray
stones inhabited by invisibly attenuate fogs of water as houses
hold always webbed glimmers, presence of families who have died
within, and so rub as you will upon the poem you are, the word
still shall be muscular with water-impulse, informing every tendon
& nerve & your way of seeing, it has come down to you from
grandmothers grandfathers mother & father, it is inescapable as time
when you twist the sinewed towel about you muffling your clean
flesh the synonym of love, somewhat muffling but not eradicating,
for in your face & eyes & hands it sings clear, and do you understand how
it is praise, love is praise, Susan, of what is, and if it be prisoned
in low earth it shall bound in high air saying like howitzers its

name and if it be scurried to & fro over cold wastes of skies yet
shall it touch with all its names blade root stone roof and if
it be locked solid at both poles there it shall say its name with
infinite unthinking purity, where it is hardest for men to live
with and even so they wrest its substance there and men there are
gentlest of any peoples where animals too go robed churchly in
white, nowhere would you escape it, for dark of night flooding on
is water and when you sleep those are strong cables of water towing
you slack through all the names you might say or take and when
you move sportive or lovemaking it is water which faucets jet & direct
flashing and when you regard children it is water becoming a warm
osmotic cell surrounded by water, and death too is a drowsing black
unmoving lake below the throats of all springs & founts whatsoever
where they draw bright energies and can gleam in the woods like
foamflowers, but you have already known water is not to fear, and
now when you take my hand absentmindedly in your cool hand I feel
bathed also, I feel washed quite brilliant, I feel rising helpless
to my mouth your name   Susan Susan   and now I do say it in praise of
you.

VI   Dead Soldiers

I remember seven floods, the worst
In 1946 when the sluice-gates burst
And logs came blundering from the paper mill,
Choking Pigeon River below Smathers Hill,
Clanging culvert pipes and headfirst fast
Into Fiberville Bridge. It wouldn't last,
Old lattice-work of peeling paint and rust.
Everyone gathered at Campbell's store just
To see how long before it broke.
                              Old man
Campbell was unabashedly drunk again.
(Not that he hadn't good cause—this time, at least.)
His house and store stood the flood-bank, yellow yeast
And black poison water already chewing
Off his lower lawn. Five big logs slewing
Down kidnapped his pumphouse. He swore in angry
Disbelief when he saw it strew in the hungry
Acids. "Sweet Jesus Christamighty Gawd,"
He said, and spat whiskey spittle at the broad
And broadening river. "Somebody ought to by Christ
Do something. A man could stand it oncet . . . but *twicet*—"

No one offering to halt the flood, he took
A drink and held his pint to the light to look
How much. Three-quarters gone. He swigged it off
One gulp, turned purple, and began to cough.
"Somebody by God ought—"
                              The only help
He got was thumping on his back for a gulp
Of desperate breath. He dropped the empty, staring

25

Morose at piebald pine and oak logs boring
Chopped butts a moment up into drizzly day
Light, dipping like porpoises, swooping away
Toward Tennessee. "Guy works and slaves and where's
It get you," he said. "A limp dick, gray hairs,
A pile of debt is all I know. You'd think
The goddam Mill would've thought—"

                              Midnight ink
Ineradicable, the flood kept swelling, blacking the rose
Garden laid back out of elm-reach where snows
Could quilt it warm. "If Elsie was alive she'd die
To see it." Dime-sized rain from the sagging sky
Dropped and he raised his startled face. "*Son*
Of a bitch." The farmers gaping him for fun
Began to mumble, thinking how more rain
Would ruin them too. If it happened again—
Having been flooded two years before—they'd have
Bank notes so deep only a Peace Valley grave
Could free them.
                              Suddenly Campbell departed the hill,
Dashed into his house, and returned ready to kill
Somebody or maybe only something, bearing
New whiskey, a .22 rifle, shells; and swearing
Rare enough to shame a rattlesnake.
Instantly he gained respect.

                              "Chrisake,
Virgil, what you doing?"

                              "I ain't going to stand
Here and not fight back what's taking my land
And house," he said.

                              "You can't goddammit shoot
A river."

He spat. "I'd like to know why not."

And so he did. Loaded, and started pumping
Slug after slug at the water rising and thumping
His house like a big bass drum. All at once
The basement doors burst open and out floated tons,
Or what seemed tons, of emptied whiskey jars.

"Lord, Virgil, did you drink all that?"

                               "Sure's
You're damned I did." He grinned. "But the goddam dead
Soldiers won't stay dead. Must be," he said,
"The goddam Day of Resurrection." And started in
Picking them off. Insensible husks of gin,
Bourbon, scotch, and moonshine sank as once more
He killed them certain. How many? At least a score
Of each, though nobody counted, struck dumb no doubt
At load on load of bottles rumbling out.
He never missed. He must have known by heart
Where each one sat on the shelf. Maybe a part
Of his crazy pride was knowing to a decimal point
How much he drank, having little to flaunt
Himself with else. Or maybe this unguessed cache
Of glassware was to him not splendid trash
But secret treasure he alone knew how
To value, now bobbing away in the fearful flow.
Anyway, he shot them to splinters, accurate
As cancer, muttering no one could quite hear what.
At last he busted them all. At last they'd never
Rise again, bright jewels in pitch river.

And now we heard a great inanimate groan,
A scream of something dying that stretched bone
And muscle in electric spasm. Enormous shriek
Of shearing iron made our knees go weak.
The bridge was falling. Drooping in curlicues
Like licorice, and shrugging up torn spews
Of shouting metal, and widening outward like a mouth

Slowly grinning to show each snagged-off tooth,
It plunged the water with a noise like the fall of Rome.
Everyone hollered at once. Gray boil of foam
And halved girders jumped cloudward between the piers,
Subsiding in a hail of bolts.

                    No cheers
Then, no laughing, but a silence solemn and deep
As church spread in the crowd like opiate half-sleep.
The great event was over; they'd finally seen
It all. A post-coital calm flushed clean
Their senses as they turned bright-glazed eyes
Toward mired roads home under purpling pink-streaked skies.

That's what I think *they* saw. But what *I* saw
Was Virgil Campbell with a meaningful slow
Smile lift his gun, and just when the bridge tumbled
He fired upon it a single shot, and grumbled,
"Better put it out of its misery."

After twenty-five murky years I still see
Him there, crazed Minuteman at river edge
With a .22 Marlin bringing down a bridge.

*

"Well, here you are at last," my father said.
"I've been looking for you." I turned my head
To find him suddenly solid in sudden dusk
Behind me, shape looming lightless, and gravid musk
Of cigarettes and wet wool standing like smoke
About him, an imminent immuring cloak
Formless. But awesome as God to a child of ten.
"Don't tell me you've got so dumb you don't know when
It's milking time." I followed him to the truck
And we went wallowing home through rutted muck.
"Virgil Campbell took a .22
And shot the iron bridge down," I said.

                                        "That's true,"
He said presently, "if you think so. I can
Swear to it he's an independent man."

And nothing else for a while. At the barn he
Added, "That must have been something to see."

VII My Grandfather Gets Doused

He hedged his final bet.
The old man decided, to get saved
You had to get *all* wet.

An early April Sunday he braved
Cold river and a plague
Of cold Baptist stares. He waved

And nodded. I saw his wounded leg
Wince at the touch
Of icy stream-edge.

Righteous clutch
Of the preacher dragged him farther in.
Maybe now he didn't want it much,

But ringed by mutely sniggering men
And contraltos making moues,
He managed a foolish unaccustomed grin

And plunged to his knees in ooze
And rush of Pigeon River.
What a bad black bruise

Of reputation! Never
In a thousand thousand thousand years
Had Davis or Clark turned hard-believer

Baptist. Weeping wormy tears
His Methodist fathers screamed
In paid-for plots. My uncles' sneers

Rose like spiritual kites. Who dreamed
Heresy lurked in his slick Sibelius-like head?
It was not seemly what he seemed.

Dead,
And grounded like a hog or horsefly, would
Be better than raving Baptist. No one admitted

It, but to be good
Was to be Methodist.
And everybody should.

Man, were they ever pissed!
He'd taken the habit of laying down laws,
So now this exhibitionist

Apostasy didn't sit so well.
And they all felt sneaky-content because
There went *his* ass to hell.

They'd togged him out in white,
And he rose from the water with a look
As naked and contrite

As a fifth-grader caught with a dirty book.
Was he truly saved at last?
Before he could take it back

They said the words fast
And hustled him to dry ground
And shook his hand with ungracious haste.

If his theology was unsound,
At least he had a healthy fear
Of dying . . . . He frowned

When he saw me gaping. A double tear
Bloomed at the rim of his eye.
In a yellow-green willow a finch sang clear

And high.
Silence seized us every one,
Standing bemused and dry.

Now O pitiful he looked. The sun
Cloud-muffled, a cold wind-stir
Brought us to compassion.

They fetched his clothes from the car;
Still expostulating,
The preacher led him to a laurel thicket where

He changed. *And changed again.* Waiting
In numb wonder, we heard his voice go
Grating.

Baptized he was. But now
He decided to be *un*baptized. Pale
Pale the preacher grew;

I thought his heart would fail.
"No, Mr. Davis, no no no." It couldn't be.
Baptism was all or not at all,

Like virginity.
He'd have to stay washed white,
Baptist through eternity.

"Well, that's all right,"
He said. "But I had no notion it *took* so quick."
His voice glared unworldly light.

Grasped his walking stick,
And saddling his armpit on his crutch, he strode,
Dragging the dead foot like a brick.

At the side of the narrow road
He turned to watch the river driving east.
(Was West Fork Pigeon *really* the Blood

Of the Lamb?) A shadow-creased
Scowl huddled his face
When a thought bubbled up like yeast:

The water that saved him was some place
Else now, washing away the sins
Of trout down past McKinnon Trace.

And now he hoisted his stoic limbs
Into the home-bound Ford. "What damn difference
Will it make?" he said. "Sometimes
I think I ain't got a lick of sense."

VIII   My Grandmother Washes Her Vessels

In the white-washed medical-smelling milkhouse
She wrestled clanging steel; grumbled and trembled,
Hoisting the twenty-gallon cans to the ledge
Of the spring-run (six by three, a concrete grave
Of slow water). Before she toppled them in—
Dented armored soldiers booming in pain—
She stopped to rest, brushing a streak of damp
Hair back, white as underbark. She sighed.

"I ain't strong enough no more to heft these things.
I could now and then wish for a man
Or two . . . Or maybe not. More trouble, likely,
Than what their rations will get them to do."

The August six-o'clock sunlight struck a wry
Oblong on the north wall. Yellow light entering
This bone-white milkhouse recharged itself white,
Seeped pristine into the dozen strainer cloths
Drying overhead.

           "Don't you like men?"

Her hand hid the corner of her childlike grin
Where she'd dropped her upper plate and left a gap.
"Depends on the use you want them for," she said.
"Some things they're good at, some they oughtn't touch."

"Wasn't Grandaddy a good carpenter?"

She nodded absentminded. "He was fine.
Built churches, houses, barns in seven counties.
Built the old trout hatchery on Balsam . . .
Here. Give me a hand."

                    We lifted down
Gently a can and held it till it drowned.
Gushed out of its headless neck a musky clabber
Whitening water like a bedsheet ghost.
I thought, Here spills the soldier's spirit out;
If I could drink a sip I'd know excitements
He has known; travails, battles, tourneys,
A short life fluttering with pennants.

                              She grabbed
A frazzly long-handled brush and scrubbed his innards
Out. Dun flakes of dried milk floated up,
Streamed drainward. In his trachea water sucked
Obscenely, graying like a storm-sky.

"You never told me how you met."

                              She straightened,
Rubbed the base of her spine with a dripping hand.
"Can't recollect. Some things, you know, just seem
To go clear from your mind. Probably
He spotted me at prayer meeting, or it could
Have been a barn-raising. That was the way
We did things then. Not like now, with the men
All hours cavorting up and down in cars."

Again she smiled. I might have sworn she winked.

"But what do you remember?"

                              "Oh, lots of things.
About all an old woman is good for
Is remembering . . . . But getting married to Frank
Wasn't the beginning of my life.
I'd taught school up Greasy Branch since I
Was seventeen. And I took the first census
Ever in Madison County. You can't see
It now, but there was a flock of young men come

Knocking on my door. If I'd a mind
I could have danced six nights of the week."

We tugged the cleaned can out, upended it
To dry on the worn oak ledge, and pushed the other
Belching in. Slowly it filled and sank.

"Of course, it wasn't hard to pick Frank out,
The straightest-standing man I ever saw.
Had a waxed moustache and a chestnut mare.
Before I'd give my say I made him cut
That moustache off. I didn't relish kissing
A briar patch. He laughed when I said that,
Went home and shaved . . . . It wasn't the picking and saying
That caused me ponder, though. Getting married—
In church—in front of people—for good and all:
It makes you pause. Here I was twenty-eight,
Strong and healthy, not one day sick since I
Was born. What cause would I have to be waiting
On a man?"

　　　　　　　Suddenly she sat on the spring-run edge
And stared bewildered at empty air, murmuring.

"I never said this to a soul, I don't
Know why . . . I told my papa, 'Please hitch me
The buggy Sunday noon. I can drive
Myself to my own wedding.' That's what I did,
I drove myself. A clear June day as cool
As April, and I came to where we used to ford
Laurel River a little above Coleman's mill,
And I stopped the horse and I thought and thought.
If I cross this river I won't turn back. I'll join
To that blue-eyed man as long as I've got breath.
There won't be nothing I can feel alone
About again. My heart came to my throat.
I suppose I must have wept. And then I heard

A yellowhammer in a willow tree
Just singing out, ringing like a dance-fiddle
Over the gurgly river-sound, just singing
To make the whole world hush to listen to him.
And then my tears stopped dropping down, and I touched
Nellie with the whip, and we crossed over."

IX   Science Fiction Water Letter to Guy Lillian

May 28, 1971

Dear Guy,

                                        It
is not quite true I said science fiction images
lack imagination. What they lack is resonance.
The usual s-f novel is as numb, deaf, and
odorless as a patient readied for surgery.
Surely imagination is sensual, truthfully
septic, like a child wallowing his dog. S-f is
self-indulgent also, but less pleasurable to
the fingers; a deliberate squeamishness obtains;
finally nothing is at stake. Intellectual,
is it? But why propound ideas no one would die
for or live with? The most unblinking hedonist stakes
at least his body. —Maybe what s-f needs is a
martyr, someone to risk his vanity for what he
believes an improbable truth. Then science fiction
could degenerate into religion, where they keep
imagination burning white as acetylene.

Please don't get me wrong. I'd be the last man to object
to a literature of paradigm. Borges I
love, and Aesop (quick chess pieces carved in animal
shapes), and the uncloudy delights of Sherlock Holmes, and
any story about unknown languages or codes.
It's not the skeleton that rattles me, but the flesh—
or want of it . . . And why are bureaucracies treated
as admirable or even necessary? Why
are there no devout women mentioned? Why do children
never starve or burn?

Trouble is, the difficulties
to be solved are never hard, the insolubles are
taken as premises. Thus, these novels cast themselves
away from myth, which possibly could justify them.
For myth originates then when imagination
struggles, falters, and finally takes a flying leap.
Id est, myth' springs from hiatus of historical
data, a need to justify present cultural
anomaly; myth is critique of lost history.
But science fiction has no feel for pastness, and at
most a high school textbook notion of cause-and-effect;
its heroes are always blatant bloody prodigies
like Patton, Napoleon, Xerxes—*always Moloch*;
vulgar pains, almost without exception, in the ass.
Which partly accounts for s-f's garish surface (when
it has a surface), and for omnipresence of blood
(its color but not its taste). —It counts suffering out.

(Right here I want to list exceptions. Injustice to
H. G. Wells, Olaf Stapledon, Poe, H. P. Lovecraft,
and *Rudyard Kipling* would be ungrateful on my part.)

In my whole file of A. E. van Vogt no one changes
his socks, or chips a tooth, or shaves. No one even farms.
Those boys are always either *thinking* (something hotstuff,
you bet) or *reacting* with split-second reflexes—
like garter snakes. Not a calloused palm in a platoon
of heroes. They've got glands, all right, of the push-button
sort, but that doesn't make them human—merely in heat.
And an absence of saints: one would expect no Ghandis
or St. Claras or Schweitzers in this most secular
of literatures—but why no Curies, Oppenheims,
Galilei? These were persons; but s-f desires
merely a set of bubble-gum-card figures: the truth's
not in it, not even a lurid truth.

Old buddy,
here I stop bitching. No use to fault stuff that never

aimed at anything much in the first place. Probably
what troubles me most is the poets; usually
everything's their mucking, anyway. They let it get
by them, all that pure data, those images, that new
access to unplumbable reaches of space-time. They're
still whining, like flawed Dylan records, about their poor
lost innocence, and the manifold injustices
continually visited upon them, and their
purple-murky erotic lives, and their utterly
horrid forebears—maybe now and then pausing to gawk
a Flower or The Sea. The heart of it is, if the
stuff's not employed by poets, it'll find *somewhere* a
position, if it has to be among the anti-
poets. Fresh wonders clamor for language, and if the
word-order is second rate, they'll take it in lieu of
braver speech. But let me tell you, Guy, this dilemma
is a fashionable oddity left over from
the '90s (Wilde, Mallarmé, & Co.). Marvell
or Donne or Vaughan wouldn't let such opportunities
rot on the stalk; they'd already have one foot moon-bound
and a weather eye out for pulsars; they had senses
alive apart from their egos, and took delight in
every new page of Natural Theology.
(If that thought is not correct, it òught to be.) And all
this material would be virgin as an unfilled
pie shell if Heinlein and Asimov hadn't got there
first, prinking hobnail-boot tracks and scattering beer cans.

I bet you've guessed it. All these too-many pages of
flaccid syllabics are apologia for my
own absolutely magnificent science fiction
novel. Of course, it's not written yet, but I've got notes,
an outline, and fairly clear notions of what I want
to say. I hope you don't expect I'll live up to what
by negative inference my ideals seem—no one
ever does. But I'd like to make anyhow a start,

the weirder the better. Counting on your tolerance,
I append a five-stress summary.

THE NOVEL:

Know ye, Lillian, that once upon this earth
Words had not the shape that now they shine in,
And men had earless only holes to balance
The wind that whooshed their heads, and a single eye
On the lefthand side blinked in the cheek. Strange
Beings, men of matter not of flesh,
Such creatures that walked when void and atom married;
And nothing then of the comforting mud that chinks
Our bones. Nor had they mouths to say or slobber.
Up and down the diamonded soil they ran,
Aimless and endless in a kind of Brownian motion.
And words lay all about the landscape, lay
Half-buried in glittering ground, or propped cockeyed
Against metallic trees . . . . For words were objects
In that crystal season, great lunking hulks
Unmanageable. Slabs of matrix unnameable,
Discrete, and silent as a birdless sky.
No one, know ye, knew what they were. The notion
Of *word* had not yet squiggled into being.
But there they were, twitchy to be discovered,
All words that in the world ever were or will.

Take "is," for example. Here was a frost-on-iron-
colored dodecahedron forty feet long
With faces unreflecting which stood at the center
Of that senseless tribal scurrying, an obstacle,
If they'd known what "obstacles" were. ("Obstacle" itself
Was a globular little pebble streaked with blue.)
Let us take "like." "Like" was everywhere,
An abrasive glinting dust bitter to taste—
Had there been mouths—cloaking all the objects

That were really words. Or think of "soul":
Small solid round cuddly boulder
You'd hug to your chest. All tongue was there:
"Tovarisch," "shantih," "amo," "Chattahoochee,"
Lying connectionless upon sterility.
No man paid them any mind.

Beyond the moon a race of beings superior
Then throve, and observed the plight of human men
With pitying hearts. *Archamens* they were called,
Of the planet *Nirvan,* which circled the deeps of Aquarius
Constellation. Flitted the galaxies
Faster than love can whisper the loins in spaceships
Constructed of intellectual soap bubbles. Knowledge
They'd gained, of the transitory and sempiternal,
And they decided to take a hand. Accordingly,
They sent an envoy, a lady who'd been awarded
Mother of the Year (on Nirvan seven
Thousand seven hundred forty days).
For her a simple task. She brought her ship
Downily to couch upon our prickly planet.
Stepped forth splendid in radiant gossamer
And took the hand of the first dumb joe who came
Along. (Later, when names came into fashion,
He spelled himself Adam.) She led him a mile
Through clanking desert to the foot of a mountain taller
Than Pisgah, hill of blue-green-gray-white flashing,
A single mineral.
                    "Now listen to me, honey,"
She said. "I'm going to say this once, so try
To get it. What you're looking at is *water.*
You understand me? This is *water. Water.*"

Brother, you shoulda been there! Obviously,
It blew that dim ember of brain he had
To highest heat. Certainly it was water.

Why hadn't he figured it out before? *Water*—
So simple a notion . . .

                              And in that instant everything
Occurred that still occurs and shall occur.
From his holey head his ears began to peep
Out, tentative as snail-horns. Featureless chin
Blossomed a mouth like a red red rose, mouth
Suffering to speak. And a second eye
Bulged brightly, setting in order the face that now
We know. He struggled; sweat suffused his form.
At last he got it out. "Water," he said.
(Or maybe "wodor" or "wat-tar" or "wazzar" or "wawa.")

And the mountain itself! began to change, rumbling
Gushy, and rippling majestic as borealis,
Finally collapsing, like jello in an oven, to liquid;
And began to search the secret veins of earth.
Everything changed! Palm trees sprang forth, and lilies.
Elephants, tigers, cows, green beans, papaya . . .
Whatever name you like to name took root,
And the world filled up with glorious language, bleating
Like a million million trumpets.

                              Our Lovely Mother,
Satisfied (almost smirking, is my guess),
Remounted her ship and starward rode off silent.
Adam didn't even notice, so joyed
He was, so battered with delight at names
Which on every flaming side struck both his eyes.

Over and over he said it: "Water. Water."
And other words: "Pomegranate. Baseball. Mouse.
Cadillac. Poem. Paradise. Cinnamon Doughnut."
When he said, "Man," everyone changed to persons
Like himself. (Except the women, of course.)

But that one word he loved, and said again:
"Water. Water. Water. Water. Water."

THE END

So there you have the main drift of it, at least. I'd be
curious to know what you think, so long as it is
favorable and congratulatory. If it's
not, you dog, don't even bother to answer

old Fred.

X   On Stillpoint Hill at Midnight

The sea driving its salt wedge
into rivers,
bridges and trees plunging bare arms
into earth,
mountains through their roots
sucking earth
up to bare spaces,
and suns overhead and moons grinding
like peppermills,
and heart's-blood searching out
every tendril in the body
and returning;
each upheaval that order is,
my stillness takes in.

My stillness a method of hearing.
Elements huddling,
stars and waters sing
a whole still note.

On this hill at midnight
I, pallidly glowing
(I glow amidst the dead),
consider how the giants went
into earth
patiently to wait themselves
into stone;
considering again how stones will burgeon
into animals, erupting to four feet
on glossy lawns,
and gnawing the ruled streets and lot corners
of suburbs

like moths devouring stripes
in a bolt of plaid.

This stillness filled with potency as a pebble
flung upward, wrinkling stars in rings.

My gaze will return from sagging
fences of the stars
and once more plummet
into my eyes.
Will return battered like
an old dory
from the mole-runs of starlight
and steep cataracts
between the atoms
and once more launch into my eyes.
Appearances shall unfasten,
the world divest of illusionary bloom
loll its doped head,
flower with wounded stem.

Then shall I see you with new eyes.
We are locked like chain
steadfast,
we are fixed while around us
creation dribbles
out the bottleneck of diminishment.
We must keep calm and admire
one another now
as stones, waters, stars,
and spaces cry out
in furious concord,
heaving unceasing the unutterable
into being.

It is the wind shall cleanse us,
I tender you promise
of the wind.

All. All is moveless if only
we lie easy on the surface-
tension of history.
Remembering how
in Plemmons' springhouse with water
tunneling fast up amid mineral
crawfish, your face
white slid like a proud steam yacht
over the cold boiling-away:
so must we cohabit
with event,
touchless with our allegiances as water-
spider's feet upon stream-skin.

We will rest simple,
we will taste with our pores
the powerful probabilities massing about
indivisible infinite motes of water
as earth sweats itself
in this springhead.
Or come with me at 6 a.m.
in the woods by the lake
(carp-slap sharp as rifle shot
through ringing silence),
where I can point one drop of dew
on sassafrass leaf
which reflects the whole breadth of dawn
gray and blue-gray.
For water, like human
history, weeps
itself into being.

We must lie careless as
these forces foment,
we also must reflect every
fire of the heavens
and the cool effortless moon

trawling our faces.
Must read too the waters clouding us,
feel soup-green billows
drifting our blood, blood
prophetic with earth, wind, and star,
seas sloshing artery walls.

Every level seeks its own water.
Water is whole because it is patient.

Mostly I dare not think it:
slow rain twitching wounds and eyelids
of murdered soldiers,
daily snail-white corpses
bloating the Mekong and Hudson,
muskrat drowned chewing his leg
in the iron purse-snap,
rivers rotting to lye where
the mill-drains vomit inky venom,
current fingering endlessly jagged steel
of sunken liners
(melting the bones of the filthy rich
to gray jelly),
aborted
babies thrust into sewer pipes: how
on the sterling upper plane
of water
we the living dance thoughtless,
steady in one place,
while in the living muscle
dead men toil
and compose their strengths.
In satin inlets of our sleep
they will surface
and like pistons swim
absolutely toward us.
They depart no painted paradise

with harps and lutes
but a dread salt Sargasso
thirsting for our green blood.

The moon, Susan, 's a-tilt now.
Let us join hands, descend
this star-bathed hill
to where the study light, the kitchen
light, corridor the dark.
Let us enter breathless our leaking house,
turn bedsheets, preparing to voyage
wherever these midnight waters
stream.

We shall not fear.

We are moving still.

XI   The River Seeks Again the Sea

Again. Deep morning.

Collect
From day, from time of stream, collect
From vagary and tic, my mind suckles your shoreless lonesomeness.
                            Susan   Susan,
Where go we now? I guess we wash towards death.
May I hold your hand?

Sometimes I look your eye to the core.
Sea I see. What promise else
Adventurous have you never?
What what what can I do burning?
We have tried our best.
We shall.

Listen, unlucky, how I see us:
The universe is bigger.
Can we belong? How do we join?
The stars come by
In tides, winds and waters peep us rancorless.
What do you wish, I wish.
No, I will also be a man.

Mind coming apart to water, searching salt springs
Of earth, or is it the sea reaching
To first fresh fingertips of water in stone in the high mountains?
What I know is, no one sleeps apart.

Ever ever
In unanimous voice we drift,
Selflessness of energies bright and blind.
We are each us. There is no me.
(I do not mind.)

The world asleep is begging us to sleep.
The world asleep
Broadens and unshapes.
What unthinkable current sweeps our grandmothers?
We shall meet again on that other shore.

We shall meet again, we shall meet
When now touchless my hand on your breast is swimming
Unfeeling wilderness of time present and past.
And now you mutter in dream and now you say
My dream.
Our life is gratefully asleep.

Never never
Would I wish to wake, except to kiss
Your dark eyelids febrile with dream.
Never will I wake your eyes.
The earth is shoving us to sea, the sea shoulders us
To another earth.
So we stand naked and carefree and holding

In the dew-fired earliest morning of the world.

Bloodfire

This is the hour when windows escape
houses to catch fire at the end of the
world where our world is going to dawn.

—René Char

I Fire Now Wakening on the River

Morning.
First light shapes the trees.

　　Behind tensed lids begins the salvo
Of silent orange curtain, little by little rising, changing
In rising to the sky-wide hem of the northern *Borealis*.
In alert half-sleep I follow upward the supernal sheer
Of burning drapery.
　　　　　Between lid and pupil
The façade of first-light comes floating.
Air-galleons of touchless fire drift above the whitened river.

How, love, in this frenzy of illuminant particles, each atom a spark,
May I you touch?
　　　　My forehead enters your shoulder
As air and flame enjoin, nothing separate,
All selfless in all as we burn together,
Ascend the air we make, wavering, visible.
We waver within one another.
The world in sunlit half-sleep is a film of fire.

It is a forest of fire suspended; the animals
That live in fire—that burning tiger, firefly and salamander, firedrake—
Observe us with their slash eyes,
See us rise in air as they rise in air,
See us twine as above a candle the yellow and red entwine.
Our bloods ascend this stalk of air like the snakes of a caduceus.
At last in fire we two are one and none.

The limits consume themselves, it is an ecstasy
Of forgetting and aspiring, how can this tight bedroom
Contain us?

(Our half-sleep of whitened waters
Rises, the river thrusts sunward
Its refracted columns. Cloud-margins the color of lit fuses.)

Or wind diving out of the sky and driving the flames forward,
Small flames like dog teeth
Biting the black circle larger, larger;
Green growth curls surly on the widening circle,
Boiled juices of poison oak smear the air a greasy window.
        This wilderness of doubt
We clear for our rough hovel, root the stump up
To lay our smooth hearthstone.

               Now shall I clutch your life
In the fitful bed. Born troublous, elusive
As the spark flown upward, you shall not now escape
My net of furious dream.

I dream your mouth gasps open unbreathing,
Your arms outstretched above your head, swimmer
Of the heated air, you launch to sound the divided deeps of void.
        This way the world was formed,
The purer spirits surged ever upward,
Shucking the gross pig-matter their bodies;
Lie glittering round the zenith like strewn glass.
Mountain and riverbed are the stacked dead husks.
The pure spirits stand among monsters and heroes,
Orion, Hercules, Cassiopeia,
And Draco and the Big and Little Bear.
And we this hour, 28 May 1971,
Are Gemini:
       the Twins, each each and the other
Like the two-colored candleflame.

Torn sheet of light sizzles in the mirror:

The seeds, ignis semina, of fire
Put forth in me their rootlets, the tree of fire
Begins to shape itself.

　　　　　　　　I have no wish to awake,
Ever to awake, to be exiled a cinder
From my globe of half-dream,
To be born stark ignorant in my thirty-fifth year.

Trees fully aglow,
I reach for clothing.

To be fresh born at thirty-five,
That is a death.
　　　　　　My flesh unburns
In coolness of morning.

II   Rimbaud Fire Letter to Jim Applewhite

That decade with Rimbaud I don't regret.
But could not live again. Man, that was *hard.*
Nursing the artificial fevers, wet
With Falstaff beer, I walked the railyard,
Stumbled the moon-streaked tracks, reciting line
After burning line I couldn't understand.
In the long twilight I waited for a sign
The world its symbols would mount at my command.

My folks thought I was crazy, maybe I was.
Drinking behind the garbage back of Maxine's Grill,
I formulated esoteric laws
That nothing ever obeyed, or ever will.
"Les brasiers, pleuvant aux rafales de givre.—Douceurs!"
I must have dreamed those words a hundred times,
But what they meant, or even what they *were,*
I never knew. They glowed in my head like flames.

Four things I knew: Rimbaud was genius pure;
The colors of the vowels and verb tenses;
That civilization was going up in fire;
And how to derange every last one of my senses:
Kind of a handbook on how to be weird and silly.
It might have helped if I had known some French,
But like any other Haywood County hillbilly
The simple thought of the language made me flinch.

So passed my high school years. The senior prom
I missed, and the girls, and all the thrilling sports.
My teachers asked me, "Boy, where you *from?*"
"From deep in a savage forest of unknown words."
The dialogue went downhill after that,

58

But our positions were clear respectively:
They stood up for health and truth and light,
I stood up for Baudelaire and me.

The subject gets more and more embarrassing.
Should I mention the clumsy shrine I built
In the maple tree behind old Plemmons' spring?
Or how I played the young Artur to the hilt
In beer joints where the acrid farmers drank?
Or how I tried to make my eyes look *through?*
—I'd better not. Enough, that I stayed drunk
For eight hot years, and came up black and blue.

One trouble was that time was running out.
Rimbaud had finished "all that shit" before
He reached his nineteenth year. I had about
Nineteen short months to get down to the core.
I never did, of course. I wrote a bunch
Of junk I'm grateful to have burned; I read
Some books. But my courage was totally out to lunch.
Oh, Fred Fred Fred Fred Fred . . .

Remember when we met our freshman year?
Not something you'd want to repeat, I guess, for still
R. worked his will in me, a blue blear
Smoke poured forth. (That, and alcohol.)
(And an army of cranky opinions about whatever
Topic was brought up.) (And a hateful pose
Of expertise.) Jesus, was I clever!
And smelt myself as smelling like a rose.

I had a wish, "Mourir aux fleuves barbares,"
And to fulfill it could have stayed at home.
But down at Duke in 1954
(*I like Ike*) it carried weight with some
Few wild men and true who wanted to write
And even tried to write—God bless them
Everyone!—and who scheduled the night
For BEER and the explication of a POEM.

Well, you recall: Mayola's Chili House,
Annamaria's Pizza, Maitland's Top Hat,
The Pickwick, and that truly squalid place,
The Duchess, where the local whores stayed fat
On college boys, and the Blue Star, the I.
P.D. But the joint that really made us flip
Sat sunsoaked on Broad St., where we walked by
Rambeau's Barber Shop.

Those were the days! . . . —But they went on and on and on.
The failure I saw myself grew darker and darker.
And hearing the hard new myths from Bob Mirandon,
I got Rimbaud confused with Charlie Parker.
It was a mess, mon vieux. Finally
They kicked me out, and back to the hills I went.
But not before they'd taught me how to see
Myself as halfway halved and halfway blent.

Jim, we talked our heads off. What didn't we say?
We didn't say what it cost our women to prop
Our psyches up, we couldn't admit *the day*
And age belonged still to our fathers. One drop
Distillate of Carolina reality
Might have cured much, but they couldn't make us drink.
We kept on terribly seeing how to see,
We kept on terribly thinking how to think.

They turned me down for the army. I wanted it raw,
I wanted to find a wound my mother could love.
("Il a deux trous rouges au côté droit.")
I wanted Uncle Sugar to call my bluff . . .
No soap. I wound up hauling fertilizer,
Collecting bills, and trying to read Rimbaud
At night, and preaching those poems to David Deas or
Anyone else I thought might care to know.

The only good thing was that I got married.
And I watched the mountains until the mountains touched

My mind and partly tore away my fire-red
Vision of a universe besmirched.
I started my Concordance to Samuel Johnson,
And learned to list a proper footnote, got down
To reading folks like Pope and Bertrand Bronson,
And turned my back on the ashes of Paree-town.

But as my father said, "Fire's in the bloodstream."
The groaning it cost my muse to take off my edge
Still sounds in my sleep, rasps my furious dream.
—Tell you what, Jim: let's grow old and sage;
Let's don't wind up brilliant, young, and dead.
Let's just remember.
                              —Give my love to Jan.
Yours for terror and symbolism,
                                            ole Fred.

28 May 1971

III My Father Allergic to Fire

My father said: "The South is in love with fire.
You're eighteen, you're old enough to witness.
Barn-burnings, house-burnings, field-burnings . . . Anything
You want to name, we'll put to kerosene.
I can't say why. Maybe we caught it from Sherman."
On Hogback Ridge he kicked the cookstove, muttering.
The cabin whimpered at the corners, December
Predawn wind ripping down off the toothy
Rock-knob mountain top.
                              "What's the matter
With the stove?" I asked.
                              "Nothing, except you've got
To show this bitch who's boss. These old wood ranges,
They ought to keep half-hot. We don't come up
Hunting often enough so this one's accustomed.
Give her a kick if you want to hear her rumble.

"Anyhow, the South and fire: in the bloodstream,
Boy. The preachers preach it; it's all they know,
How we'll fry like bacon in the afterlife.
Maybe hellfire is good for the South, a kind
Of purgative. We could use a lot of that."

"What you talking?"
                              He grinned; and broke two eggs
Into a panful of grease. "One kind of fire, though,
Will make me ill to the vomiting point. My belly
When they burn those crosses comes up into my mouth."

Eighteen years of gingerly middle-class
Bringing-up prevented me. Newspaper
Accounts were all I knew, and ever would.
"The world," I told my dad, "is full of bastards.

Choosing the Klan to get dog-sick about,
That's like choosing a particular beggar's-lice."

"Because I joined the Klan." His voice was quiet
And dark and empty as an abandoned well.

"You joined the *what?*" (Trying not to giggle.)

"It's true, though. Not that I offered harm to black folks
Or dressed up in percales . . . I was nine,
And messing around behind the packhouse, the way
A kid will mess around. Here came my brother
And a fellow I'd never seen. What made me duck
Underneath the packhouse and sit in the soft cool dust
With my chin propped on my knees I couldn't tell you.
I wasn't spying on my brother, anyhow
Not really spying—maybe like Leatherstocking.
(I'd read a fair-sized pile of Fenimore Cooper.)
I sat fiddling my fingers in the dust, breathing
The cool, and heard—nothing. Not one word.
Just a blurry clutter of older voices.
And all I could see were pairs of cut-off legs.
That got plenty boring. When I crawled out
They grabbed me, started asking what I heard.
Nothing, I kept saying, but they were scared."

"Of what?" I asked.
                    "Of themselves," he said. "What else?
They were kids like me playing in the dust.
They might have been pirates or cowboys if they hadn't caught
The germ. But they'd talked themselves into the Klan,
And they were taking it serious as death.
You would too, given the time and place . . .
So I had to be initiated. They
Thought that would make them safe, me being one
Of them, whatever it was they thought they were."

"Initiated how?"
                    He turned and sat down

At the table. "They said some mumbly-jumbly I didn't
Understand, and gouged some blood from my thumb,
And burned the cross on me."

                              "'Burned what?"

                                        "The cross."
He undid his shirt halfway. "Took kitchen matches
And heated the flat of the pocket knife blade
And branded my hide. Look here." Peeled back two layers
Of undershirt and bared his shoulder to me.
"It hurt like fury. They didn't like it either,
But this was the pinch they'd conspired themselves into."

"I don't see anything."

                        "It's forty years.
Look close."

              I stared into my father's skin.
A little pimple in a square of gray-pink flesh.
I peered as into a fog that held my future,
And no cross glowed there silver, no cross at all.
"Can't you see it?" He pleaded like a child.

My father's innocent shoulder I almost kissed.

"Can't you—?"

              "I see it now," I said. "It's smaller
Than I thought it'd be. It's really awfully small."

He breathed in deep relief and buttoned his shirt.
"Maybe now it is, but there was a time
It felt as big as the moon."

                        "That time is past."

"No time is past they made you shed blood on."

"The time for frying eggs is past," I said.
He opened his eyes. The cabin was full of smoke.

IV   Feverscape: The Silver Planet

Tensed lids or open eyes. Landscape the color of Jesus-words
in the testament, or color of sun on the gold-red edge.
Umber fire in my head the books and fevers drove me upon.

No illness passed me by; I lay in the sheets and boiled.
Firetree of illness spread over me,
I saw red sky through stained-glass leaves.

In the red wall of illness I saw Blackbeard
with his face afire, Dimaggio's bat like a flamethrower;
and the soldiers and cities went red as maple leaves.

I swallowed the Second World War off the greasy *Lifes*',
photos of Hitler and the cordwood dead, waiting for Dr. Payne
to beckon me in to his chisel and meat saw.

Always above me the bronze angels of sickness hovered
like church bells, faces hidden, hands hidden.
The sheet was a snow of fire. I saw fever take on flesh.

My visitor most frequent was the Planet of Silver Fire.
Size of a basketball between bed and ceiling. Its color
was the color of beveled glass. The rainbow of fear.

Planet within whose continents I saw libraries
of Holy Bibles melt to gas, continents of ash-scab like
griffons and fern-faced witches thirsting for my marrow.

The oceans of the Silver Planet glowed with the horrible fishes
in the encyclopedia: Dragonfish, Sea Viper, Lamprotoxu,
Chiasmodon, like threads of tungsten in light bulbs.

And at its poles the shiniest fires: vast leaping
coronas fingered the medicine space I suffered in,
scrawled prescriptions on the tipped ceiling.

White tentacles of camphor-smelling flame the Silver
Planet lashed me with, each wound an alien word,
arms of fire scribbling me in the steamy bed.

I died of all those illnesses I didn't die of.
Whole duchies of my spirit went to inhabit
the stainless fires of the Silver Planet.

So I know well what sickness comes trembling over
the edge of the world. It is the great and
gleaming wolf spider with cunning caution.

And have become your stranger tarrying here,
your special leper.
Taste me to taste somewhat that Planet.

Yet still we must believe somewhere
exists the true cool dark forbidden us.
We want to wash our faces in it.

Too long we have bared our backs, we
have bent our heads beneath the cruel silver fire.
The nerves keep smoldering but never catch.

V   Firewood

Flame flame where I hit now, the cat is scared, heart
red in the oak where sun
climbed vein by vein to seek the cool
wedge hard where I strike now and rose
leaves drop off as if ruin of cloud on cloud
fell, heart of red oak strips to sunlight,
sunlight chopped like this to pie chunks,
like this, solid as rock cleft rock, rock
riven by vein and vein, ah if it were all
so easy, to hit it & see it & feel it
buck & come clean salmon colored,
so clean I would eat it, this neat chop
takes down the spine of the world, page of
sun stripe opens, bright flesh of oak
flashes its rivers, easy to read firelight
in the new flesh, though sometimes not
so easy to break, deaf thunder of the hammer
fraction by fraction nudges the wedge in,
blow on blow not yielding at all until
28 strokes tear a jag
of shadow-lightning across the grooved
round top, black lightning slash through
the years, and the ringing of hammer and wedge
deepens from alto to baritone, rag bark falls
off and the naked grubs curl up in agony
of sunshine, or these joints the *marriage
vow* joints, what God has joined together
let no man put asunder, where the wedge not
an inch in an hour of hitting goes in and the
arms quiver exhausted, sweat soaking the crotch

of the twist shorts, and nothing, this baby
simply don't give & don't even promise just
like the nice girls back in high school, remember?,
going to be married to this flint round of
wood forever, till finally fin;al;ly it bust loose
to show the dagger-shaped knot hid in the
heart of it, black and ochre and dark red, looks like
a trawler steaming up the stream of veins,
or a stubborn island in the colorful river, what
secret part of my life is it? so resisting and
so in tight upon itself, so bitter bitter hard
until at last torn open shows that all the secret
was merely the hardness itself, there's no true
shame worth hiding but some knot of hurt
hardly recalled, yet how can I say it
is not beautiful this filigree of primaries,
its form hermetic in the flow of time the
rings transcribe, I will set it down amid
the *perfect things,* alongside the livid day
lilies here and the terrapins I brought home
as a child & kept in the cool basement
with the arrowheads and alongside Don Larsen's
Series game in 1956, for
anything so entirely itself must have value even
if it's only in the exercise of seeing it whole,
also hard are these big lengths of walnut, must
be 4 good feet across here & the wedge goes
in like a 6 penny nail & splits it no more
than a nail, have to start the other wedge here
in the little tear you couldn't mail a postcard
through, and just keep thumping away, 12-pound
sledge hefts heavy off the downswing, then bit
by bit like a political scandal it uncloses
itself except at the rugged heart the tendons
won't let go, hold on like hinges and the angle
so tight the axe head can't get in to slice clear,

have to on my knees rassle it like a hawg,
and as at last it tears I feel in my breast the
tearing, letting go reluctant as paying death
taxes, and this one piece is free though my fingers
bleed and the huge rest of the half just squats there
waiting, a whole armory of pain as dumb as stone,
but let me tell you, *Log,* godammit I already see
you stacked in the andirons blazing like a porno
starlet & as cheerfully garrulous as a general
store porch whittler, I see the life of you, yellow
red and orange and blue & hasting your dark gasses
starward, on the silverblue night splaying a new tree
shape, tree of spirit spread on the night wind,
& sifting upward to the needle pricks of
fire those bones of the heroes and monsters (Orion,
Draco, Cassiopeia, Karloff), the sweaty red
roots of this tree sizzle in our fireplace, the
ghostly arms of it embrace the moon, the lancet
glance of the star pierces its leafage, this tree
in our fireplace is the sun risen at midnight,
capillaries of heat light lift out the chimney,
the rose trellis of stars is afire, sun reaches
homeward again to the *vacant interlunar spaces,*
chimney is its shrunk trunk & pins our dwelling
to the earth and to the stars equally, this spirit
trunk in the chimney is the spine of the world,
world of darkness that huddles to the windows
& flattens its face against the panes bloodthirsty
for those entangled roots of flame and each hour
leans more heavily inward as the fire goes blue
in the rootlets & the embers heap to the shape of
a walnut meat as this grand fire begins to ponder
the problem of mortality and its arms among the
stars grow more and more tenuous, that's how it
is true the cold dark will tear our tree of fire
away complete, the hearth will cool & blacken,

the seeds of fire will blink dark one by one, but
before that and *even so* and *after all* it shall have
been a fierce glory of color, it shall have been a
goddam Hallelujah of light and warmth, warmth
enough to read by, we can read books, we can
read each others' faces, we can read the chair the
table the wall, read everything that is except the fire
itself giving us heat to read by, we can
even half read the dark that sucks the fire away
& swallows, hearth being dug out of earth &
overpowering entropy of earth clouds from the
beginning the wild root mass of fire, it was sun
jammed into dirt that raised this tree, Lucretius'
seed of fire ignis semina is seed semina mortuis
(*dirt we rose from, dirt we'll never forget*)
of death in that same split second, moment
split by the man's hand hard as an iron wedge
hammered into the seam between the double
eternities of zilch zip zero (& that's how man
goes forward; hits himself on the head with a hammer),
or maybe not, helluva proton here, the wood the
up quark, wedge the down quark, and man is don't
you know it buddy the *strange* q., so perhaps
the nuclear shell will hold longer than I might
have thought until until until that roaming
puddle of gravitons, a winter's night the black
hole, comes this way striding & yanks the tree
of light elongate like a sunny licorice down
the drain, yet since once I cleaned the well I'm
given to understand that here is the well that cleans
the universe and I believe it sure for the shadow
of that hardest knuckle of matter casts forward
into the flesh of light itself, see here?, this black
knar monadic and unmoving in the steady pour
of red and yellow honey of sun meat, who
knows, maybe the knot is the man or the man's

will angry against the stream of time, or is it as
they say, *the eye,* and here in the furl something
that is our unguessable double, tripledark other
punches his headbusting language through, wants
to tell us that in the antiuniverse Rimbaud is
right, that the poet encoding *can* transform all
germens with an incantatory perception of what's
what or what's supposed, the vatic will can at
the bottom trifle with an energy or two & make of
every tree that stands a *Christmas tree,* Christmas
on Earth, though even as I recall the beautiful
manifesto my faith flickers & dwindles, we are not
born for the rarer destinies only for the rarest,
we are born to enter the tree of smoke, backbone of
the world of substance, born to smear our life stuff
against the zodiac, & as I take down in matter
the spine of the world & will send it up again in
spirit a feeling that these things are so indelibly
correct overtakes me that I must pause over the half
driven wedge & water it with the sweat of my
armpit & watch my neighbor's beige terrier
ambassador of funky accidence snuffle the loud
mouthed day lilies and the tattered chips of log
and finally my sopped socks & bound away through
the fence gate as if everything round the wood
pile here were just too bleeding metaphysical
to be borne & I watch the wily jive of his
stub tail go away with something I admit like
green envy thinking why cannot my animal
wallow within himself content, why can't simply
the act of breaking the wood be plenty
enough, just the feel of it, stark augenblick
of hammer head and wedge head and then in
a while the gorgeous ripe rip of the log
broken open, sound of a watermelon dropped two
stories down, and the good ache at the bottom

of the spine and the good pain of the pocked
blister worn open the good sweat salt in my eyes,
just this and no more: the body's hungry
response to iron and wood: a primal hedonism: this
will be sufficient when I come to the wisdom
my neighbor's beige terrier possesses: but man in
his fallen state is condemned to split the tree
with his intellect all alert and doubtful, mind
fingering the restive chunks comes up empty handed,
there is I tell you in the texture of this log that
which taunts the mind & calls it simpleton and
idiot and to which the poor old browbeaten mind
acquiesces saying, All right, matter, you got me, I'm
horsewhipped & buffaloed, does that satisfy you, &
nothing happens except that matter retains its smirking
hardness & just sits there half split with how many
eons of pain stored up in the other half & says
nary a word & doesn't need to, we know what it
means or intends to mean: that when man and nature
got married they agreed never to divorce although
they knew they could never be happy & would have only
the one child Art who would bring mostly grief
to them both: but that *man always forgets* so
when here he comes with his sledge and his wedge and
an edge in his voice saying, Matter, I'm gonna
kick your ass all over this universe, matter has only
to sit quiet thinking, My man, never you heard of
passive resistance?, why that's the secret of the
world, Mexican stand off is the closest you'll get
to the heart's heat heart of the heart,
why don't you try the lotus position or the string
quartet or something equally restful, for never has
mere fever got you anywhere or me either come
to that, we could make such beautiful silence
together if only you'd slow down & shape up & let
things as they are have their guiltless pleasures,

and man replies saying unto matter, Wassamatta
you, you talking commie now all this strike talk,
I been sentenced doncha know to create reality
by the sweat of my brow, Bible sez so, take
that you hard weird pinko freak, and with this I
bring the hammer down and the wedge the old
hearthurter doesn't even *budge,* and easily it could go
on like this forever since it forever has, better take
a moment's cigarette & watch the rose petals
drop off and the day lilies scramble toward the
11 o'clock sunshine just the way this severed
tree once yearned & clutched toward, I will
sit on this log & breathe bluegray smoke (but where
shall I sit when once this flesh is spirit?) &
try to think where next to hit & smite & bash &
knock it, maybe just once on the wedge one more time,
& the wedge goes in like semen, easy as sea
current into the estuary river, & the log breaks apart
to disclose what? flesh! more flesh! flesh the
same as before and the river-clean smell of opened
flesh comes at me as the annunciation to Mary,
attar of matter, a radiance of sweet rib of wood
no man has seen before, I'm washed in the blood
of the sun, the ghostly holy of the deep deep log
interfuses me till I feel whole here and almost
cool but it doesn't come easy, I'm
here to tell you that

VI My Grandfather's Church Goes Up

(Acts 2:1-47)

God is a fire in the head.
—Nijinsky

Holocaust, pentecost: what heaped heartbreak:

The tendrils of fire   forthrightly tasting
foundation to rooftree   flesh of that edifice . . .
Why was sear sent   to sunder those jointures,
the wheat-hued wood   wasted to heaven?
Both altar and apse   the air ascended
in sullen smoke.

     (It was surely no sign
of God's salt grievance   but grizzled *Weird* grimly
and widely wandering.)

     The dutiful worshipers
stood afar ghast-struck   as the green cedar shingles
burst outward like birds   disturbed in their birling.
Choir stall crushed inward   flayed planking in curlicues
back on it bending,   broad beams of chestnut
oak poplar and pine   gasht open paint-pockets.
And the organ uttered   an unholy *Omega*
as gilt pipes and pedals   pulsed into rubble.

How it all took tongue!   A total hosannah
this building burgeoned,   the black hymnals whispering
leaves lisping in agony   leaping alight,
sopranos' white scapulars   each singly singeing
robes of the baritones   roaring like rivers
the balcony bellowing   and buckling. In the basement
where the M.Y.F.   had mumbled for mercies
the cane-bottomed chairs   chirruped Chinese.
What a glare   of garish glottals

rose from the nave   what knar-mouthed natter!
And the transept tottered   intoning like tympani
as the harsh heat   held hold there.
The whole church resounded   reared its rare anthem
crying out Christ-mercy   to the cloud-cloven sky.

Those portents Saint Paul   foretold to us peoples
fresh now appeared: bifurcate fire-tongues,
and as of wild winds   a swart mighty wrestling,
blood fire and vapor   of smoke vastly vaulting,
the sun into darkness   deadened and dimmed,
wonders in heaven   signs wrought in the world:
the Spirit poured out   on souls of us sinners.
In this din as of drunkeness   the old men dreamed dreams,
the daughters and sons   supernal sights saw.
God's gaudy grace   grasped them up groaning.
Doubt parched within them   pure power overtaking
their senses. Sobbing   like sweethearts bereft
the brothers and sisters   burst into singing.
Truly the Holy   Ghost here now halted,
held sway in their hearts   healed there the hurt.

Now over the narthex   the neat little steeple
force of the fire   felt furiously.
Bruit of black smoke   borne skyward
shadowed its shutters   swam forth in swelter.
It stood as stone   for onstreaming moments
then carefully crumpled   closed inward in char.
The brass bell within it   broke loose, bountifully
pealing, plunged   plangent to the pavement
and a glamour of clangor   gored cloudward gaily.

That was the ringing that wrung   remorse out of us clean,
the elemental echo   the elect would hear always;
in peace or in peril   that peal would pull them.

Seventeen seasons   have since parted
the killing by fire   of my grandfather's kirk.

Moving of our Maker   on this middle earth
is not to be mind-gripped   by any men.

Here Susan and I   saw it, come
to this wood, wicker   basket and wool blanket
swung between us,   in sweet June
on picnic. Prattling   like parakeets
we smoothed out for our meal-place   the mild meadow grasses
and spread our sandwiches   in the sunlit greensward.
Then amorously ate.   And afterward
lay languorous and   looking lazily.
Green grass and pokeweed   gooseberry bushes
pink rambling rose   and raspberry vine
sassafras and thistle   and serrate sawbriar
clover and columbine   clung to the remnants,
grew in that ground   once granted to God.
Blackbirds and thrushes   built blithely there
the ferret and kingsnake   fed in the footing.
The wilderness rawly   had walked over those walls
and the deep-drinking forest   driven them down.

Now silence sang: swoon of wind
ambled the oak trees   and arching aspens.

In happy half-sleep   I heard or half-heard
in the bliss of breeze   breath of my grandfather,
vaunt of his voice   advance us vaward.
No fears fretted me   and a freedom followed
this vision vouchsafed,   victory of spirit.
He in the wind   wept not, but wonderfully
spoke softly   soothing to peace.
What matter he murmured   I never remembered,
words melted in wisps   washed whitely away;
but calm came into me   and cool repose.
Where Fate had fixed   no fervor formed;
he had accepted   wholeness of his handiwork.

Again it was given   to the Grace-grain that grew it,
had gone again   gleaming to Genesis

to the stark beginning   where the first stars burned.
Touchless and tristless   Time took it anew
and changed that church-plot   to an enchanted chrisom
of leaf and flower   of lithe light and shade.

Pilgrim, the past   becomes prayer
becomes remembrance rock-real   of Resurrection
when the Willer so willeth   works his wild wonders.

VII   Firewater

Beneath the hairy hams hung from the hooks
Virgil Campbell talked in his grocery store:

"I just got back from the hundredth anniversary
Of Clay County. I have kinfolks that way,
They asked me out to see the spectacle.
The local politicians—just to give you
A notion—were calling themselves *town fathers.*
So then I know something's bound to happen.
If I had fathered a town I wouldn't brag
About Hayesville. I mean, there's a matter of pride.

"First off, the usual stuff. Speeches crammed
To the gullet with lies; sorghum-judging,
Jam-judging, cake-judging, quilt-judging; ribbons
Handed out to the grandmaws and the livestock.
And then the square dance contest. (I got to say
The Hiawassee Stompers can flat out clog some . . .)
I was rolling with it right along,
Had me a laugh and a sip or two . . .   J. T.,
They had them a beauty queen. That gal was *healthy,*
I'm here to tell you, and ought to season out
As comfortable as a split rail fence
And keep as many varmints off your ground . . .
Maybe my taste is running sophisticated,
I've lived too long in the wicked city of Pigeon Fork.

"The main attraction, besides the knife- and fist-fights,
Was the Clay County Hundredth Grand Parade,
Celebrating their most famous products.
—Now what's Clay County famous for?"

                                        "Moonshine,"

My father said.
                    "And everybody knows it,
But who'd've thought they'd parade it on the street?
Damn if they didn't. They went up Standing Indian
And told Big Mama to build a model still
And put it on a wagon and ride with it.
Ten years they've been trying to prosecute
That woman for running shine, and out of the blue
They come up hat in hand to ask her sweetly
To waltz it down Main Street in broad daylight.

"And she said Yes. The notion had to tickle her
Once they got past her mean suspiciousness.
So there she was. I saw her. Swear to Jesus.
Sitting in a rocking chair on a wagon
By the cooker, and the copper worm
Strung down behind her, and smoke just boiling out
Pretty as you please. A cat would've by God laughed.
Big Mama weighs close onto three hundred pounds,
But the Hayesville Beauty Queen didn't sit prouder.
She gave a special wave to the deputy sheriff.
Grinning grinning grinning like she'd stole
The courthouse weathervane. Rocking and grinning and rocking.

"Behind her came the Briar Hill Bluegrass Band
On another wagon pulled by a one-eyed mule.
That's what I thought, the way he drew to the left.
But then he'd pull the other way; and began
To kind of hop and stagger. At last he gave a lurch
And lay down in the traces and went to sleep.
Somebody hollered out, 'That mule's drunk!'
Sure enough he was. Drunk as an owl,
Just from breathing the smoke that was pouring out
From Big Mama's *model* still. The music stopped.

"Because they'd caught her at last. After all those years . . .
But what are they going to do? They'd invited her;

They begged her to do her stuff, and so she did.
Here came the deputy. 'You're under arrest,'
He said—but smiling so the crowd would think
It was part of the act. Big Mama's boys stood up—
Wearing phony beards, barefoot with beat-up hats,
Just like the hillbillies in the funny papers—
And threw down on the deputy three shotguns.
Whether they were loaded I don't know.
He didn't know. Except Big Mama's bunch
Nobody knew. Fire don't flame as red
As that man's face. He waved them along, smiling
Till his jaw hurt. It'll take a month to relax
That smile away. They drove on around the square,
Getting their money's worth, leaving behind
That passed-out mule for the deputy to have fun with.
And went on home, back to the rocks and laurels."

"Okay," my father said, "it's good to know
The eternal verities still hold their own,
That poverty and whiskey and scratch-ankle farming
Still prop the mountains up."

                              "But it ain't that way,"
The old man said. "Big Mama's quit running corn,
Except for home use. Ain't no profit in it,
With the price of sugar up and the appetite down.
Growing these Merry Widow cigarettes,
That's where they make their money."

                                        "Kind of a shame,
Tradition dying away. The funny papers
Will come to be all anybody knows."

"It ain't that bad. I know one high-grade still
Still making. If you'd care to have a snort."

"Why not?" my father said. "Time keeps grumbling on.
Let's drink us a drink: here at the end of the world."

VIII   My Father Burns Washington

Money money.
During Hoover's deep
Depression we did not have any.
Not enough to buy a night's good sleep.
My parents went to bed in the grip
Of money and dreamed of money.

We heard them walk
The resounding rooms below,
My sister and I, heard them stalk
The phantom dollar and ghostly dime. "Where to
From here?" The question always grew
Heavier in the dark.

My sister and I
Clutched hands. Money would climb
The stair, we thought, and, growling, try
The doorknob, enter upon us furiously.
Its eyes like embers in the room,
It would devour all time.

The morning brought
Chill light to lined faces.
My father spoke of other cases
Worse than ours: Miller Henson's place was
Up for sale; Al Smith had fought
And lost; Clyde Barrow got shot.

Christ, how he tried!
One job was farming, another
Teaching school, and on the side
He grubbed for Carolina Power & Light.
Came home one night to our driven mother,
Lay back his head and cried

In outrage: "Money.
Money. Money. It's the death
Of the world. If it wasn't for goddam money
A man might think a thought, might draw a breath
Of freedom. But all I can think is, Money.
Money by God is death."

Her face went hard.
"It won't always be
This way," she said. "I hear them say
It's beginning to get better." "You'd take the word
Of that political blowhard?
Old Franklin Pie-in-the-Sky?"

"Well, what's the use
Of carrying on like this?"
"It soothes my feelings." My father rose
From his chair and menaced a democratic fist
At the ceiling. "I refuse,"
He said, "to kiss their ass."

"J. T., hush!"

And now he noticed me
Shriveling in the doorway. A flush
Of shame for language spread his neck. He
Pulled me to him. A woolen crush
Of jacket rubbed my eye.

Then stood me back.
"Don't worry, hon, we'll make
Out all right . . .   But it's still true
That thinking of nothing but money makes me sick.
A man's got better things to do
Than always feeling low."

"We'll make it fine,"
She said. She tried to grin.
"I can understand how tired

You get. And I get weary to the bone.
Even so, I think—" She bit the word.
Her temper had pulled thin.

"Don't think," he said.
(That became my father's
Motto.) *If I had my druthers:*
That's all thinking amounts to now. It withers
The will to think like that. We need
To think what *can* be had."

The argument
Seemed to die away.
He stared before him, restless silent
Despondent; we stood waiting for him to say
Whatever would ease his soul, turned flint-
Hard and moveless and dry.

He fished a green
Flimsy one dollar bill
From his pocket. "I've got it down
The philosophers are right: the root of evil
Is paper. This one at least won't kill
Another desperate man."

He got a match.
We listened, frozen in time,
To the ugly inarticulate scratch
And watched the tender blooming of the flame.
"I never figured on getting rich."
Revenge was sweet with doom.

He lit the single.
When the corner caught
We felt a minatory tingle
Advance our skins. Had he truly taught
Us freedom, amid our paralyzed mangle
Of motive and black thought?

It made no more
Lovely a fire than any
Other fuel: a flame and a char
Of paper. We couldn't think of it as money
Burning but as oxidized despair
Climbing the indifferent air.

He wept as it burned,
Then flung it down and ground
The corner out and, ashen, turned
To face my mother who smiled and frowned
At once. Like a beaten child he mourned:
"Mother, will it still spend?"

IX Burning the Frankenstein Monster:
Elegiac Letter to Richard Dillard

It is Henry, as everyone knows, who's really the monster,
    Not the innocent wistful crazy-quilt of dead flesh
We remember as being in love with flowers and children like flowers.
    It's the will made totally single which frightens us,
Monstrum horrendum, informe, ingens, cui lumen ademptum:
    Virgil's misshapen eyeless one-eye gone mad
And disturbing the fabric of ongoing time. —You were right, Richard,
    What I mostly ripped off from Rimbaud was the notion of fire
As symbolic of tortured, transcendent-striving will.

(But *The Inkling* is long out of print, bemuses not even my mother.
    Let it smolder to ash on whatever forgotten shelf.)

Why must poor Karloff be born out of fire, and die, fire-fearing,
    In the fire? Is he truly our dream of Promethean man?
Does he warn us of terrible births from atomic furnaces, atomic
    Centuries, shambling in pain from the rose-scented past?
Having been burned and then drowned, reversing the fate of Shelley,
    The lame monster brings back upon us the inverted weight
Of the romantic period. Whose children we are, but disinherit,
    Stranded in decades when all is flame and nothing but flame.

And my vividest memory: light first seen by the monster, pouring
    Through the roof peeled back little by little, at last
Bathing in splendor the seamed unlovable face with its stricken
    Eyes; and the creature in agony uplifting his hands,
Whimpering gutturally, hoping to be drawn up like water vapor
    Into the full forgiving embrace of the progenitor Sun.
What wouldn't *we* give to undergo in our latter years the virgin
    Onslaught of light? To be born again into light,
To be raised from the grave, rudimentary senses unfolding like flowers
    In a warm April rainfall . . .   But then they reseal the roof;

Little by little his hands drop again to his sides and the brightness
　　Lapses in stone-colored eyes, his mind huddles forlorn.

Henry is watching in barely controlled hysteria, thinking
　　Thoughts inarticulate, biting his rag-like hands.
He is a child of the lightning also, of the flash unrepeated
　　Revelation which blasts and creates in an instant, all.
Flash he must follow to destruction, before us melting whitely
　　To madness. Let him then marry, let the wine be fetched
Out of the family cellars, the servants giggling like tipsy chickens
　　When the baron proposes his toast: "A son to the House
Of Frankenstein!" —Has he forgotten that Henry already has fathered
　　A son given over to the care of Fritz, dark spirit of Earth?

Fritz is unbearable. Crazy perhaps and certainly turned evil
　　By reason of fear, it's he who teaches the monster to fear,
Perverting the light to a means of torture. This troll always scurrying
　　Upstairs and down with a torch in his hand is reduced
Finally to shadow, to shadow hanged and splayed on the prison
　　Wall. This is justice, of course, but it horrifies the mad
Doctor, the sane doctor, and every one of those whose consciences
　　Whisper: *The fault is yours, for the dead must bury the dead.*

Return to the lake where the two abandoned children are playing:
　　Here is no murder, no trial of death upon life.
Entrancement of naked simplicity washes both the bright faces;
　　Pastoral daisies, the currency of joy between two,
Float in the water; the monster is struggling to utter first laughter.
　　Now the sweet daisies are gone, and the hands that had held them ache,
Tremble with joylessness. Suddenly metaphor is born to the injured
　　Criminal brain, and he plucks a final white bloom,
Launches it silvery drifting. The death of all flowers forever
　　Is accomplished. From moist green ground he has plucked his own death.

Nuptials broken . . . The father in silent dry-eyed accusation
　　Brings to the wedding the single drowned flower of death . . .
(Notice in horror films, Richard, how weddings impendent on science,
　　Knowledge unborn, recur. In *Dracula, Curse*

Of the Demon, in Freund's *The Mummy,* in Hillyer's *Dracula's*
Daughter, in *Dr. Jekyll and Mr. Hyde.*
Hearing "the loud bassoon," but prevented—until we listen
    To Salvation's full passion—the church, we stand aghast.
Faith calls to faith, but our faith must be earned from terror, consummate
    Love must be thirsted for, light must be wholly desired.)

White-gowned Elizabeth sees in the mirror the wayward monster
    (Calendar girl who confronts a medieval death's-head);
Hears the low growl, a deep rasp as if earth were tearing in tatters;
    Obligingly faints. And the monster her bridegroom lifts
Her over the threshold, through door after door, but the ritual is empty.
    Only one union is Karloff permitted: to wed
Terribly the flames, to return to the trauma of being fathered
    Once again, conceived in the raging delirium of fire.

    Father and son, they are bound to a wheel of crazed fire.

Father and son, with one instant of recognition between them:
    Jagged and hungry the gears that ponderously chew
The circle, and father and son for a moment pause to examine.
    "You who brought me into this world what have you done?"
"No. Never you I sired but a healthy longed-for imago."
    "I am but I and I come now to claim my birthright."
"Born of my will from the grave, for you this world holds nothing."
    "Maker and monster we shall not die apart."

Richard, this world is ever the world the fathers fashioned.
    Right and the right to be right belong to dreams
Not as yet come into flesh. The courageous monsters perish
    Always alone, and yet always in a final light
Glorious and stark. As the hilltop mill is always burning,
    Raising its arms of clean blaze against the stars.

X Bloodfire

(Of the fire-martyrs of the war: the immolated and self-immolated)

Siblings scorch-eyed and aloof
Now you lie across the wars
Emblazoning a worst reproof
Of promises broken, burning scars
Of an inhuman politic.
Now floods into the plundered heart
Sick pity for the querulous sick,
The garrulous dead. No more apart
You lie entwined in rank blood.

I recognized you from the first.
Struggling in your sweat-soaked bed
You wept, your head ablaze with thirst
For absolution. Where was none.
The bitter uproot shouting throng
You saw frustrate upon your screen,
But knew you never could belong
To another army, however right
In motive, cause, and claim, however
Righteous it appeared on sight.
Yours was the holy importunate fever.

Now to my door the papers bring
Your names or the names of towns that die.
New promises flourish now; late spring
has brought the Pentagon's newest lie.
But nothing's new. The same machine
Toils on, grinding out the stats.
Westmoreland's photogenic grin
Assures: more gold braid on more hats.

In every politician's tattle,
Bloat exigencies of shame,

You heard within his words the rattle
Of M-14s, the skin-tight flame
Of phosphorous grenades, strafing
Of paddies, unmanned hospitals leveled,
Children murdered past believing.
In sleepless fear of God you groveled.

And rose to mornings of fresher lies,
Of newspapers smeared with the greasy smirk
Of a thief whose principles green flies
Wouldn't shit on in his hatefilled dark.
Your heart fell ill at the sun coming up.
Coffee gagged you. You rode to work
Past faces that had lost their grip,
Each feature a featureless mark.

Trembling I read the same accounts.
I too suffered, I was there.
I watched them kill for brownie points.
My sleep too dissolved in fire.

Terror engorged us. Television,
Little gray cage with its black joke,
Brought us our latest Sense of Mission
And the new installment of *Gunsmoke*.
That was *our* light at the end of the tunnel.
And in our TV dinners we found
Hands and eyeballs in a neat little bundle.
Who among us was not stoned?

Here I stopped. Here I turned
Back to the books that nurtured me
When I met evil first, learned
An implacable philosophy.
But you went on. Striving striving
In the lightless void to know
What best to make of guilty living
In a decade without love or law.

When everything had gone so far
The center was past the edge, you fell
To pieces, let their dirty war
Possess you. You invited hell;
Decided not another dawn
Would see you powerless to say
The sentence someone had to say:
We now divorce this filthy game.
Then in the bluest hour of day
You died, and rose again in flame.

And still we die.
And rise in flame.

XI   Bloodfire Garden

It is the disease
necessary to know God.
It is the heat
in the animal calling to animals,
              Take me into your world of blade and rock
help me return   to when the sun
first struck off in fury
the boiling planets.

It is the fever reaching down
to the fluid core of earth,
connection
with first daybreak lapping
the unstarred walls of time,
connection
with beginning.
                        It is
desire.
It is the skin
sniffing the skin of the other,
and convulsion of heart's-blood
when the woman turns from watching
through the window, unloosens
the halter-strings,
steps forward gravely, and on
the bedside table
sows a handful of bobby pins.

It is the flame which obsesses silence.

              Love, in the fire we are
whole again,

our atoms driven and
interlocked as heat in air;
after the slow blind tracings
we leap up scarlet in fire,
star-shudder overcomes our limbs when we strain
one another against fire-mesh,
straining our figures elongate,
toe-tip to fingertip,
like candleflames in the new wind
sprung at twilight.

        This is the gleam
I starved after when
at twelve years I saw
in some nestle on the mountains at midnight
the hunters' campfire
blinking   blinking
and walked in the dark to the edge
of the river,
and could go no farther,
but looked there upon
Orion
sliding the water calmly.

Now you warm me.

The snap.
It is the snap I remember
in the fresh-turned late-March garden.
    My father by the chicken
wire fence scythed short
the blackberry vine,
scribble scribble scribble
raked up in barbarous heaps,
his flint hands
steady in solid arcs across.
We put it to torch.

Clean clear
flame against mauve sunset.

Now I have come to do
the thing my father has done.

Earthsmoke
mauve in late mauve light.

The snap:
it is the sound
of shackles broken,
ice-fracture under the weight
of the mountain, clap of cut glass
coming apart, the far-off
report of oak break.
. . . Writhed in white fire.
Thorn-points firing,
sizzle on the hard
vine ribs purple green
oiled and red-streaked
frying lattice
of dry bones.

I prayed then by the thorn fire.

I went stark sane, feeling under my feet
the hands of blackberry fire
rummaging
unfurrowed earth.
At that hour in shadowy
garden ground
the ghosts began again to take flesh.

(And in the west murky corner the poison
wild cherry we girdled
to kill.)

        Love, after the snap
and the deep shudder

a cool invisible smoke goes up
from our bodies, it is grateful
prayer, sigil
of warm silence between us.

In this garden our bed we have burned
down again to the ghost of us,
green Aprils collide
in our blood.

Burnt-off, we are being prepared.
The seeds of fresh rain advance,
wind bearing from the south,
out of the green isles
of Eden.

Wind Mountain

Io venni in luogho d'ogni luce muto,
  che mugghia come fa mar per tempesta
  se da contrari venti e combattuto.

—Inferno

I came to a place entirely hushed of light,
  But rumbling like a tempest out at sea;
  The winds fought up and down, this way and that.

I   Dawn Wind Unlocks the River Sky

Early half-light, dawnwind driving
The trees.

      Wind ravels the scribble of vague clouds,
Fingers the Primavera glass curtain at sill-corner and bellies
It forward, here is my galleon-sail, I can voyage where I whither;
And do not. I push more deeply my face,
Love, to your breast.
Your small breathing harbors me. *Bedroom curls and uncurls with breath*.
Just as the curtain, curling, uncurling, is free to voyage in arabesque,
Not leaving its true place. The small breathing of earth
In our window delivers me the houses and trees, souls aswoon in wind.
Spirits drifting on the dawnwind like sleep-smoke, bonfire
Smoke.

      First sun in the glass curtain dyes it with fire,
                    It is a fire in air,
     It is a fanfare of pure spirit, prelude, aubade.

                        Do I now
Desire you harshly?
No, it is the false desire of fresh morning, my body seeks limit
Merely, curb and margin, wind-plunged.
It is a half-bitter floating in the sea of spirit,

This sea of music,
Passacaglia to every ocean, I am swimming your skin
Of touchless fire and earth-salt. Wind drives me forward like
The spider's doily, anchored at corner and corner and corner to the
Domestic shapes: black hairbrush like a sea urchin, cologne bottle,
Hairpins and comb, deodorant can,
The mirror like a burning window.
                  (Bedroom fills now
            With the aria, Rossini, of blue jay and stinksparrow.)

How the world was formed:
Wind huddled together from every quarter the dead men in it,
Wistful spirits in a gang chained lamenting to the elements,
      Elements carried from the Four Quarters by the East Wind,
By Auster, and Zephyr,
And by rapacious snaketailed Boreas.
Suffering of spirit, suffering of elements,
In one mass.

            My birthday, Year Thirty-Five,
May 28, 1971,
Is tumbling the dawn awkwardly as a broken boxkite, slenderest of twines
Holds it to me, it is Anybody's Birthday, the whole world is born again
In the morning flush of loosed wind-spirit, exhalation
Of fire-seed and gusty waters and of every dirt, Birthday sails on streams
Of atoms, freshening now the breeze in the Solomons and by Greenland,
Brilliantly invading the spicy Virgins.

Fire coming apart now to wind, earth
Divides to rivers, the world of waking shoves me bodyward.
How may I retrieve my spirit where it twirls
In the glasswalled caves of wind? Speech of morning,
Dawnwind driving the trees sunward, it is
Your breath, love, caught back pulsing in your throat where you swim
In the spirit sea, where the inspiration of your bright hair
Flows on the pillow, your bright hair a river
Of fire in early sunlight.
            The pillowslip blood-warm
With breath, the little flame of blood kindles the bedroom.

            I rock now out of the air, out
Of the pure music of absence. In the companioned bed
I retake my body, May 28, 1971.

            Time time time
To rise.
Put your pants on, Birthday Boy, the trees are
Wide awake. The shining net of dream plunges to earth,

Earth rises out of air to greet my flesh.

II The Highest Wind That Ever Blew: Homage to Louis

Music is the world over again.

—Schopenhauer

Ever, ever in unanimous voice we drift:
But not you, baby, not you, Satchel-Gator-
Dippermouth. Punch them pepper lead-notes,
Louis. Ride it, fiercemeat, yon and hither.
Birthday morning I put the record on.
Hot Five, hot damn. What a way to never
Grow old! I couldn't count how many times
You saved my life.

               Tuning my tiny Arvin,
I'd gasp to glimpse through the mindless crackle one gleamiest
Corner of a note you loosed. Once more tell us
About Black Benny and Mary Jack the Bear;
Red-Beans-and-Ricely-Ours, *all ours*,
Let's hear the Good News about Fats Waller.
"You got millions in you and you spend
A nickel": that's what the Message is, okay,
I hear you, shall I ever understand?

What's in that Trumpet is the Tree of Life,
The branches overfreight with canteloupes,
Peacocks, mangoes, and nekkid nekkid women.
And all around the tree a filigree halo
Like a silver lace mantilla. And limb to limb
Zip little silver birds like buckshot dimes,
Kissing and chucking each other under the chin.
Curst be he who worships not this Tree,
Cause you S.O.L., baby   I mean
You   outtaluck . . . It's summertime forever,

Believe to your soul; and this is the River of Jordan.
Everyone was born for a warmer climate
And a jug of wine. You born for it, sweet mama,
And me, and even the blackbox boxback preacher,
He born for it. Up on the Mountain of Wind
I heard in the valley below a lonesome churchbell
Calling home, home, home, home,
And the last swell of the hymn dying at sunset.
Everywhere in your trumpet I heard that.
I'll follow it like a fire in air, I will,
To the purple verge of the world.

                                               Rain aslant the wind,
The cozy lovers wind their wounds together.
The weepy eaves peep down into the rooms.
Wind and water drive against the windows
Like a black blind moth in the dark. They sigh
And settle and snuggle. A lemon-colored sun
Warms their innermosts, memory
Of the trumpet-bell uplifted like a sun
Where they'd paid a buck to see the greatest man
Who ever lived, man playing with fire
In air, pursuing his soul in a hovering sun;
Had a tune would melt the polar cap to whiskey.
This dreamshot sun the mellow lovers dream,
It warms them amid each other, the rain goes cozy.

And me too, man, I had me a woman livin
Way   back o' town.
Would wait till the blue-gray smoke of five o'clock
Came down and fetch my bourbon and Beechnut chewing gum
Along the cindery railroad track, counting
The chemical raw smells the paper mill
Dumped into the Pigeon, and the railroad ties.
From tie to tie I whistled *Potatohead Blues*,
Even the clarinet part. It made me happy.
It made me nostalgic for that present moment.

I could have walked like that forever, I could
Have snagged the ballhoot freight to New Orleans
And clung to the windy boxcar singing, *singing*.
I could have lugged my trombone and learned to learn . . .
I learned, anyhow . . . There's something in the woman
More than in the horn to teach you the blues.
Yet still you need the tune, it fixes a pride
On the joy of Traveling Light, there's courage in it.
Father Louis had told me all already.

What's whiskey without the jazz?
Nothin but gutache, nothin to look back on.
Whiskey alone don't fill you that honeysuckle
Sunlight in your vein, it ain't the gin
That makes you shine. It's the man in the cyclone of flame
Who keeps on saying *Yes* with a note that would light
Up the Ice Ages. He's the silver sunrise
In the pit of the body, dawnwind jiving the trees.
Thoreau was right: morning is moral reform,
Gimme a shot. And please play *West End Blues*,
I need to hear the wistful whippoorwill,
To hear the railroad ties hauling the lovers
As they walk down the line, walk down the line
With nineteen bottles of whiskey in each hand,
Going to meet the woman and hear the man.

I've had the warm May nights in the feathery grasses,
Wind poling woozy clouds across the moon,
And the glare light slicing out of the honky-tonk,
Oblong light with a frizzly shape of woman
Troubling its center, one hand on her slouch hip,
Trumpet-flutter in the jukebox behind her
Like a pinwheel of copper fire. She watched the moon.
She too knew that something pulled between them,
The moon and trumpet revolved on a common center
Of gravity which was—where? who? when? how?
Which was *some*where and some*thing*, mystical

But surely palpable, a hungry force
Obtaining as between sharpeyed lovers.

Fire's in the blood, my father told me; wind
Whips it forward, seizing every atomy
In the veins till bloodfire, bloodfire takes the body
Whole, jerks the form of a man along
On that windriver bloodfire, helplessly
A new creature in the Planet of Green Night,
Half funky animal, half pure music,
Meat and spirit drunk together under
The cotton moon. And not one man alone,
Ever, but everyone in reach of the trumpet:
An armada of fireships destroying themselves
To essence pure as wind in the fever nighttime.
Papa Louis Armstrong has refashioned us
For our savage reverend assault upon the stars.

III Second Wind

The day they laid your Grandfather away
Was as hot and still as any I recall.
Not the least little breath of air in hall
Or parlor. A glossy shimmering July day,
And I was tired, so tired I wanted to say,
"Move over, Frank-my-husband, don't hog all
The space there where you are that looks so cool";
But it's a sin to want yourself to die.

And anyhow there was plenty enough to do
To help me fend off thoughts I'd be ashamed
Of later. (Not that ever I'd be blamed.)
The house was full of people who all knew
Us from way back when. Lord knows how
They'd even heard he died. And so it seemed
I owed them to stand firm. I hadn't dreamed
There'd be so terrible many with me now.

I'd fancied, don't you see, we'd be alone.
A couple growing old, until at last
There's one of them who has to go on first,
And then the other's not entirely *one*.
Somehow I'd got it in my mind that none
Of the rest of the world would know. Whichever passed
Away would have the other to keep fast
By, and the final hours would be our own.

It wasn't like that. I suppose it never is.
Dying's just as public as signing a deed.
They've got to testify you're really dead
And haven't merely changed an old address;
And maybe someone marks it down: *One less*.

Because it doesn't matter what you did
Or didn't do, just so they put the lid
On top of someone they think they recognize.

All those people . . . So many faces strained
With the proper strain of trying to look sad.
What did they feel truly? I thought, what could
They feel, wearing their Sunday clothes and fresh-shined
Prayer-meeting shoes? . . . Completely drained,
For thoughts like that to come into my head,
And knowing I'd thought them made me feel twice bad . . .
Ninety degrees. And three weeks since it rained.

I went into the kitchen where your mother
And your aunts were frying chicken for the crowd.
I guess I had in mind to help them out,
But then I couldn't. The disheartening weather
Had got into my heart; and not another
Thing on earth seemed worth the doing. The cloud
Of greasy steam in there all sticky glued
My clothes flat to my skin. I feared I'd smother.

I wandered through the house to the bedroom
And sat down on the bed. And then lay back
And closed my eyes. And then sat up. A black
And burning thing shaped like a tomb
Rose up in my mind and spoke in flame
And told me I would never find the pluck
To go on with my life, would come down weak
And crazed and sickly, waiting for my time.

I couldn't bear that . . . Would I ever close
My eyes again? I heard the out-of-tune
Piano in the parlor and knew that soon
Aunt Tildy would crank up singing "Lo, How a Rose
E'er Blooming." —Now I'll admit Aunt Tildy tries,
But hadn't I been tried enough for one
Heartbreaking day? And then the Reverend Dunn
Would speak . . . *A Baptist preacher in my house!*

That was the final straw. I washed my face
And took off all my mourning clothes and dressed
Up in my everyday's, then tiptoed past
The parlor, sneaking like a scaredey mouse
From my own home that seemed no more a place
I'd ever feel at home in. I turned east
And walked out toward the barns. I put my trust
In common things to be more serious.

Barely got out in time. Aunt Tildy's voice
("Rough as a turkey's leg," Frank used to say)
Ran through the walls and through the oily day
Light and followed me. Lord, what a noise!
I walked a little faster toward where the rose
Vine climbed the cowlot fence and looked away
Toward Chambers Cove, out over the corn and hay,
All as still as in a picture pose.

What was I thinking? Nothing nothing nothing.
Nothing I could nicely put a name to.
There's a point in feeling bad that we come to
Where everything is hard as flint: breathing,
Walking, crying even. It's a heathen
Sorrow over us. Whatever we do,
It's nothing nothing nothing. We want to die,
And that's the bitter end of all our loving.

But then I thought I saw at the far end
Of the far cornfield a tiny stir of blade.
I held my breath; then, sure enough, a wade
Of breeze came row to row. One stalk would bend
A little, then another. It was the wind
Came tipping there, swaying the green sad
Leaves so fragile-easy it hardly made
A dimpling I could see in the bottom land.

I waited it seemed like hours. Already I
Felt better, just knowing the wind was free once more,

That something fresh rose out of those fields where
We'd worn off half our lives under the sky
That pressed us to the furrows day by day.
And I knew too the wind was headed here
Where I was standing, a cooling wind as clear
As anything that I might ever know.

It was the breath of life to me, it was
Renewal of spirit such as I could never
Deny and still name myself a believer.
The way a thing is is the way it is
Because it gets reborn; because, *because*
A breath gets in its veins strong as a river
And inches up toward light forever and ever.
As long as wind is, there's no such thing as *Was*.

The wind that turned the fields had reached the rose
Vine now and crossed the lot and brushed my face.
So fresh I couldn't hear Aunt Tildy's voice.
So strong it poured on me the weight of grace.

IV My Mother Shoots the Breeze

Hot horn hand in my face is all,
The old days. Not that I'm not glad you honor
Daddy and Mama by remembering.
But it wasn't eggs in clover by any means.
To belong like that to Old Times, you belong
To cruelty and misery . . . Oh.
I can't say just what I mean.

Whenever they talk to *you* they leave out hurting.
That's it, everybody hurt. The barns
Would hurt you, rocks in the field would bite like snakes.
And girls have skinny legs, eaten up
By rocks and briars. But I knew always a man
Was looking for me, there was a man would take me
Out of the bottom cornfield for my soul.
My Mama sent me to Carson-Newman College
And the University of Tennessee.
I came back home a schoolmarm, and could watch
Out my first grade windows women chopping
Tobacco, corn, and rocks in the first spring heat.
Two years before, and that was only me
There chopping, but now the pupils said me Yes Mam.
When I read Chaucer they learned to call me Mam.
I'd go back home and milk the cows and grade
A hundred papers. I'd have milked a thousand cows
And graded papers till my eyes went stone
To hear them call me Yes Mam before my Mama.
I taught how to read and write my first grade class
Of six-year-olds and big farm boys and grandmothers.
I'm not humble I was schoolbook proud.

First time I met your Pa he took my slip
Off. "Miss Davis, I want your pretty slip,

If you've got one loose about, for my Science class."
He was going to fly them Benjamin Franklin's kite.
I went to the women's room and squirmed it down
And sneaked it to him in a paper bag.
Under the table at lunch he grinned like a hound.
That afternoon he patched the kite together
And taught them about Electricity.
"Touch that, boys," he said, "if you want a shock.
We've got Miz Silverside's silk panties here."
(Jake Silverside was our Acting Principal.)

But I knew better what I couldn't say
And giggled like a chicken when that kite
Sailed up past my fifth period Spanish window.
I don't know what to tell you how I mean,
But I felt it was me, seeing my slip
Flying up there. It was a childish folly
But it made me warm. I know there's pictures now
Of people doing anything, whatever
Only a doctor could think of, but my slip,
Scented the way that I alone could know,
Flying past the windows made me warm.
J.T.'s the man I want, I thought, *because
He'd do anything* . . . And so he would.

But wouldn't stop . . . Everyday two weeks
In a row he ran that kite up past my window,
Long after he had worn Ben Franklin out.
It's time to show that man that I mean business,
I thought, it's time we both came down to earth.
The very next day I borrowed my daddy's 12 gauge
And smuggled it to school under a raincoat,
And when that kite came past me one more time
I propped and took my time and lagged and sighted
And blew the fool out of it, both barrels.
It floated up and down in a silky snow
Till there was nothing left. I can still remember

Your Pa's mouth open like the arch of a bridge.
"Quit troubling us maiden girls with your silly Science,"
I said, "while we're learning to talk to Mexico."

And one month later, after we were married,
He still called me Annie Mexico.

So. You're the offspring of a shotgun wedding,
But I don't blush about it much. Something
Your father taught me: *Never apologize,
Never be ashamed, it's only life . . .*
And then he was fired for creating life
From alfalfa in a jar on a window sill.

But look, I've told the story that was fun,
And I didn't mean that. What I meant to tell you:
It was hard, hard, hard, hard,
Hard.

V   The Autumn Bleat of the Weathervane Trombone

The Guernseys lift calm brows in the thistly pasture,
What must they think? that some distuneful lovesick
Paramour is moofully wooing? Cows,
Don't sweat it, it's only Fred with his battered sliphorn
Woodshedding a Bach partita on the barn roof.
This edgy October breeze is a freshener,
Don't let it teeter me to lose my toehold,
I'll tumble in the cowlot and bruise my brass.
Johann, thou shouldst be living at this hour,
You'd bust a gusset; if only the Philharmonic
Were here to listen, they'd hire me in a trice.
Is this the way Teagarden started, think you?
He must've started *some*where, so must I,
So must we all.
                    First winter's behind the mountain.

Like the spirit-shapes of great gold plums
The blown tones of the yellow trombone float
Over the fields, their wobble takes on shimmer,
There's something in air in love with rounded notes,
The goldenrod's a-groan at the globèd beauty,
These are the dreams of seeds, aspirations
Of sheeted mica, Ideal Forms of creek-glint,
Sennet and tucket of beech-leaf in its glowing,
Embers of poplar within the sun-warm crowns,
The eyes-in-air of blissful Guernseys, glass eyes
Full of the hands the little yellow hands
Of autumn drifting where they drift in blue,
Blue first-cool, the bluegold music of autumn,
Half sleep, half harmless fire, halved buttermoons,
Bring me my trombone of burning gold, bring me

My harrowing desire, bring me power
To float the cool blue air at the hinge of the year,
These notes not purely born, no, but take
A purity from air and field and sky
As they boat the wind-alleys like happy balloons,
Impure world taking purest shape in the
Bubbles of breath Bach-blown, O those golden
Fermatas, can you see them nudge and brother
The last yellow tomatoes sunning themselves
On the wilted vine, and snuggling down with the pumpkins
And bloodfire bellybloated candyroasters,
The thirty-second notes in tricky clusters
Like bunches of grapes are bunches of blue grapes,
And the chromatic eighth-notes emerge like apples,
Late-sweet streaky slightly flattened apples,
The solid apples that build their nests as high
As ever Earth can reach in the waltzing tip
Of the gnarly witchyfingered ragbark tree,
The tree in the pasture where the Guernseys wait for windfall
Patiently as the Ice Age at the Pole
Because they know an early Boreas
(Rapacious snaketailed) will bring the plunkers down,
O Susan Susan you should've been there when
The cows ate up the apples,
There's nothing quite so *musically* percussive
As the molar gronchle of apple in cow-maw,
And it wasn't was it? only apples they crunched
But some loose sixteenth-notes of J. S. Bach
Mixed in with apples shining in pasture grass,
And let's suppose that now they think this tree
The Tree of Knowledge, they've tasted the apples of music,
Talismans, and shall they ever be the same?
Hell no. They dance all night till the barns come home.

The sun is hatching the world, what new creature
Will emerge? So what, I'm hatching the barn,

I'm your setting hen with the baroquest cluck,
And what new creature will emerge? Aren't barns
The larval stages of dragons, clattery shaleskins?
Before the Fall goes down we everyone
Of us shall be new animals as strange as snow.

Yellow yellow is the color of time. The land
Is bearing itself to rainbow's end, pot
Of gold overfloods the burnt-off delta of summer,
What a dazzle of driftage, what dribble of daft
Storms the skin of the eye, I'm surfeit to bursting,
Have mercy, October, my eyes have eaten all,
I'm rich to the ears, my buttons are each in danger,
O take this table away I've gluttoned on honey,
Honey the heavy gold of time bronze bees
Have hived in the apple belly of the sun
Where all the Hallelujah candles are lit
And the Birthday Boy is momentarily
Expected, is being garnered in like corn.
In the afterlife of Sun I'll meet George Garrett,
The Golden Wiseacre, and what you think he'll tell us,
Uncle Body?—A lie, of course, some furious
Giggly tale of sex & sin & salvation,
We'll laugh our mortality to death, we'll laugh
Our frailty off . . . My fancy anyhow's
That poets after the loud labor of their lives
Are gathered to the sun, they speak in flame
Forever without erasure, they lie a lot,
Where else could all that hot and light come from?
They'll all be there, Adcock and Applewhite,
Whitehead and Tate and Jackson and Watson and Keens,
Morgan, Root, and Cherry, and Godalmighty
The very thought of it makes my ears hammer.
Trapped in a burning eternity with a herd
Of poets, what kind of fate is that for a handsome
Lad like Truly-yours-ole-Fred?

Corkscrewing

The wind, there goes a leaf of tulip poplar,
Saffron mittshape, one poet's been cast from heaven,
It's too much love of earth that draws him thither,
Bondage of toadstool, the sere the yellow leaf
His fate is sealed, he drives to mineral
Where the tree may root him out again,
The flesh the earth is suits me fine, Nirvana
A sterile and joyless blasphemy.
Give me back my blood, there's mud in it.

O yes, Uncle Body, I'll fly with thee to rootlet
And root, we'll swim come spring the tree's resounding
River-trunk, and fan our flashy shape
In green out where the squirrels are whittling toothpicks.
Take corpus after death? I wouldn't mind,
Identity can stuff it but give me Stuff,
This world's longest loaf of dirt's the staff
Of life, O Death come unbaptize me soon,
My grandfather and I never uncovered
The final source of West Fork Pigeon River,
Wonder does it burst from the solid rock
Or comes it blubbering up from the eyes of dead men?
Whichever never mind, we want to see.

Wind-river, river of flesh, spirit-river,
Fever-stream, all these the Ocean of Earth.
Let's disport it, you and I.
Can hardly wait to swim from Singapore
To Hermeneutics and through the Dardanelles
To Transcendentalism, back through the Straits
Of Hegel right on to Greasy Branch close by
Wind Mountain, look out! the perilous Falls
Of Relativity, whew that was close,
Huh-oh now we're utterly becalmed,
The existentialist Dead Sea's a mush
Of murk, help help I'm boring, ah all right,

Here the pure sweet waters of Music open
Upon a picnic wilderness of light.
Around the World in Eighty Tractates aboard
The good ship Wittgenstein, how's that grab you,
Uncle Body? How now? Asleep again,
Old lunker? Never Aquinas rages your blood,
Never up for a sweaty set of Spinoza,
Never wanted to hike with me the slopes
Of stony Heidegger? Come on, we'll pitch
Our tent tonight under the shadow of Plato.
Where's your sense of landscape got to?
If you don't take care, old hoss, Spirit's gonna
Leave you lonesome behind, then where'll you be?

No don't tell me, I never wanted to know.

But the cleanest way to travel would be to ride
One of these untenable trombone tones
Out upon the bluebleached air, forgetless
Air of crystal, steering the golden note
Over the yellowing fields until in tang
It disappears, dream-bubble's silent pop,
And lets us slide the effervescent atoms
All by ourselves, look Ma I'm flying no hands.
No feets no nothing. Nothing but eyes and taste buds
Skating the Mirror of Blazing Razors, the Eyeball
Of the Clarity of Transcendental Acids,
Lindy would envy our *Spirit of St. Francis*,
We could fly from here to Chuang Hzu's dream.

A Wilson cloud chamber I think it now,
This globe of sunswept blue, this blueblown
Note aloft in its hour of polished silk,
A chamber alert to every Cosmic Ray,
Every sizzle-streak of energy
Indeterminate unreckonable,
Every little tic in the lymph of the world;

For music reflects refracts makes visible
The hail of impulse Nature keeps tossing over
Her shoulder, sprinkle of feckless seed, heat,
Light, ray-quiver, sound, every wealth.
Entropy too keeps coming by, of course,
But nothing here except when the trombone note,
Sighing, deflates like a golden bubblegum.

I've got a slightly different Big Bang theory:
In the beginning was the Trombone—somewhere,
Somehow—and on its own it blew a true
And bluesy A, and here came rolling that note
Through Chaos, vibrato rich and round as a grape
Of Concord, O what a parable note was sounded!,
And us, we innocent children, we kinds of germs
Of music, on the outer skin of that note crawling
In helpless wonderment. And that's our fate,
We've got to tune and turn the music ever.
So I'll straddle the barn and lip the exercises,
Improve my embouchure and wiggle my slide
Till I get a somewhat humaner-looking lover
Than these bored Guernseys. Girls! girls!
Where are you? Don't you hear Fred's lonesome trombone
Mating call from the highest point in the valley?
You wouldn't let the music of this world die.

Would you?

VI   My Father's Hurricane

Like dust cloud over a bombed-out city, my father's
Homemade cigarette smoke above the ruins
Of an April supper. His face, red-weathered, shone through.
When he spoke an edge of gold tooth-cap burned
In his mouth like a star, winking at half his words.

At the little end of the table, my sister and I
Sat alert, as he set down his streaky glass
Of buttermilk. My mother picked her teeth.

"I bet you think that's something," he said, "the wind
That tore the tin roof on the barn. I bet
You think that was some kind of wind."

"Yes sir," I said (with the whole certainty
Of my eleven years), "a pretty hard wind."

"Well, that was nothing. Not much more than a breath
Of fresh air. You should have seen the winds
That came when I was your age, or near about.
They've taken to naming them female names these days,
But this one I remember best they called
Bad Egg. A woman's name just wouldn't name it."

"Bad Egg?"

           He nodded profoundly as a funeral
Home director. "That's right. Bad Egg was what
I think of as a right smart blow,
No slight ruffling of tacked-down tin.
The sky was filled with flocks of roofs, dozens
Of them like squadrons of pilotless airplanes,
Sometimes so many you couldn't even see between.
Little outhouse roofs and roofs of sheds

And great long roofs of tobacco warehouses,
Church steeples plunging along like V-2 rockets,
And hats, toupees, lampshades, and greenhouse roofs.
It even blew your aunt's glass eyeball out.
It blew the lid off a jar of pickles we'd
Been trying to unscrew for fifteen years."

"Aw," I said.

        "Don't interrupt me, boy,
I am coming to that. Because the roofs
Were only the top layer. Underneath
The roofs the trees came hurtling by, root-ends
First. They looked like flying octopuses
Glued onto frazzly toilet brushes. Oaks
And elms and cedars, peach trees dropping
Peaches—splat!—like big sweet mushy hailstones.
Apples and walnuts coming down like snow.
Below this layer of trees came a fleet of cars:
T-models, Oldsmobiles, and big Mack trucks;
And mixed in with the cars were horses tumbling
And neighing, spread-legged, and foaming at the mouth;
Cows too, churning to solid butter inside.
Beneath the layer of cars a layer of . . . everything.
What Madison County had clutched to its surface
It lost hold of. And here came bales of barbwire,
Water pumps, tobacco setters, cookstoves,
Girdles shucked off squealing ladies, statues
Of Confederate heroes, shotguns, big bunches
Of local politicians still talking of raising
Taxes. You name it, and here it came.
There was a visiting symphony orchestra
At Hot Springs School and they went flashing by,
Fiddling the 'Storm' movement of Beethoven's Sixth.
Following that—infielders prancing like black gnats—
A baseball game about five innings old.
The strangest thing adrift was a Tom Mix movie,

All wrinkled and out of order. Bad Egg
Had ripped the picture off the screen, along
With a greasy cloud of buttered popcorn."

                                         "Wait,"
I said. "I don't understand how you
Could see the other layers with all this stuff
On the bottom."

                            "I was coming to that," he said.
"If it was only a horizontal stream
It wouldn't have been so bad. But inside the main
Were other winds turning every whichway,
Crosswise and cockeyed, and up and down
Like corkscrews. Counterwinds—and mighty powerful.
It was a corkscrew caught me, and up I went;
I thought I'd pull in two. First man I met
Was Reverend Johnson, too busy ducking candlesticks
And hymnals to greet me, though he might have nodded.
And then Miz White, who taught geometry,
Washing by in a gang of obtuse triangles.
And then Bob Brendan, the Republican banker, flailing
Along with his hand in a safety deposit box.
Before I could holler I zipped up to Layer Two,
Bobbing about with Chevrolets and Fords
And Holsteins . . . I'm not bragging, but I'll bet you
I'm the only man who ever rode
An upside-down Buick a hundred miles,
If you call holding on and praying 'riding.'
That was scary, boy, to have a car wreck
Way up in the middle of the air. I shut my eyes . . .
But when I squirted up to Layer Three
I was no better off. This sideways forest
Skimming along looked mighty dark and deep.
For all I knew there could be bears in here,
Or windblown hunters to shoot me by mistake.
Mostly it was the trees—to see come clawing

At me those big root-arms—Ough! I shivered
And shuddered, I'll tell you. Worse than crocodiles:
After I dodged the ripping roots, the tails,
The heavy limbs, came sworping and clattering at me.
I was awfully glad to be leaving Layer Three."

"Wait," I said. "How come the heavy stuff's
On top? Wouldn't the lightest things go highest?"

"Hold your horses," he said, "*I was coming to that*.
Seems like it depended on the amount of surface
An object would present. A rooftop long
And flat would rise and rise, and trees with trunks
And branches. But a bar of soap would tumble
At the bottom, like a pebble in a creek.
Anyhow . . . The Layer of Roofs was worst. Sharp edges
Everywhere, a hundred miles an hour.
Some folks claim to talk about close shaves.
Let them wait till they've been through a tempest
Of giant razor-blades. *Soo-wish, sheee-oosh*!
I stretched out still on the floor of air, thinking
I'd stand a better chance. Blind luck is all
It was, though, pure blind luck. And when I rose
To the Fifth Layer—"

                    "Wait," I said. "What Fifth?
At first you only mentioned four. What Fifth?"

"*I was coming to that*," he said. "The only man
Who ever knew about the Fifth was me.
I never told a soul till now. It seems
That when the hotel roofs blew off, Bad Egg
Sucked a slew of people out of bed.
The whole fifth layer of debris was lovebirds."

"Lovebirds?"

                    "Lovebirds, honeypies, sweethearts—whatever
You want to call them."

"J.T., you watch yourself,"
My mother interjected.

                               "I'm just saying
What I saw," he said. "The boy will want
The truth, and that's the way it was . . . Fifty
Or sixty couples, at least. Some of them
I recognized: Paolo and Francesca,
And Frankie and Johnny, Napoleon
And Josephine; but most I didn't know.
Rolling and sporting in the wind like face cards
From a stag poker deck—"

                                 "J.T.!" she said.

"(All right.) But what an amazing sight it was!
I started to think all kinds of thoughts . . ."

                                 "Okay,"
I said. "But how did you get down without
Getting killed?"

                         "*I was coming to that*," he said.
"It was the queerest thing—"

VII In Parte Ove Non E Che Luca

From Circle One I came to the more narrow
    Second Circle, lightless, lashed, that place
    Resounding with lament of barren sorrow.

And there smack in the doorway sits Minòs,
    Horrible creature, who with an animal snarl,
    Judges whom he clutches so much dross.

I tell you, when the misfortunate soul
    Comes before him, *it confesses each*
    And every sin. The Connoisseur of Hell

Then assigns it to its proper ditch
    In the inferno, counting up however
    Many times round him his tail will reach.

A multitude before him stands forever;
    They come in single file before the bar
    To confess, and then to hear the judge deliver.

"Say you! who come to this Flophouse of Fear,"
    Minòs, setting momentarily
    Aside his duties, so addressed me here:

"Do you know what you are doing? Are you so free?
    Don't let yourself be fooled by the ample doorway."
    My guide told him: "Hush up your hue and cry.

"Where my friend goes you truly have no say;
    His way is willed where Will and Way are one.
    And that is all the explanation due."

And now the notes of lamentation
    Batter my ears, for I have come to the platte
    Of sighs, locale of true perdition.

I came to a place entirely hushed of light,
　　But muttering, as at sea we hear a tempest.
　　The winds fought up and down, this way and that.

The storm infernal with never any rest
　　Still drives the spirits onward with brute force
　　Tipsy, and never ceases to molest.

Up they go to the very edge of the Course
　　Of Ruin, complaining, lamenting, aghast.
　　For them the Word Divine is sheer remorse.

Into this pain the lovers of flesh are thrust,
　　All those who gave their human reason over
　　To the delicious fever of carnal lust.

There here, here there, yon-hither, lover and lover,
　　Hopeless of the comfort of coming together,
　　Of satisfaction. In torn air they hover.

As starlings at the onset of cold weather
　　Flocking take wing upon the winter sky,
　　So here, the human birds all of a feather.

And like the cranes who always make their way
　　Flying a single long unbroken line,
　　And crying stridently their broken cry,

Shadows were carried toward me on this wind.
　　I said, "Master, can you discover
　　For me who they are, so driven and blind?"

"The first you see is that notorious lover
　　Whom all will readily recall because
　　He kissed and told. His name is Casanova,

"The proud Giacomo. But the sturdy laws
　　That govern here hold him obedient
　　And helpless in this wind without surcease.

"Yet still he's harried on by his penchant
　　For conquest, never to be satisfied;
　　Always always he wants to, but he can't.

"And there, if you'll observe the other side,
   Flies one who's ordered under the Laws of Iron
   And on the whirlwind must forever slide.

"His noble name is George Gordon, Lord Byron,
   Who with his verses claimed to have seduced
   Two hundred women of Venice and environs.

"Now see to what a state he is reduced!
   When you return to Earth be sure to tell
   The boys, that *he who gooses shall be goosed*.

"The next of those you see in this loud hell
   You'll know for certain," he said. "Without dispute
   The horniest creature alive since Satan fell.

"James Dickey his name, the Poet in the Cowboy Hat,
   Whose greatest fame is propositioning
   Every woman from here to Ararat.

"No one will deny the man can sing;
   But also no one will deny that ever
   And ever he is after that one thing.

"*Deliverance?* His ceaseless thirst for beaver
   May show him sometime what that word implies.
   Some husband with a knife may him de-liver."

"Master, wait!" I said. "I recognize
   From childhood the round form, the red face
   Of Virgil Campbell, one of my father's cronies.

"May I not hear what brought him such disgrace?"
"Of course," he said, "I'll bid him to this place:"

VIII   Three Sheets in the Wind:
Virgil Campbell Confesses

Tell you, J.T., the way you see me now,
A solid by God citizen, ain't how
I've been always thought of. There was a time
I lived as raunchy as any wild boy come
Down off the mountain top, guzzling jar
On jar of whiskey, and zooming a souped-up car,
And chasing after women dawn to dawn.
It never came to mind I might slow down,
Or might as well, since there's no way I'd ever
Have it all, that there's a drowning river
Of moon out there and a river of women too.
I wasn't taking good advice, you know—
Not that plenty didn't come my way.
My woman Elsie made sure to have her say
And she'd leagued up with a hardshell Baptist preacher.
Lordy, how I hated to hear that creature
Stand up and witness at my busting head.
Then Elsie'd say again just what he said
Just one more time. It was no sweet cure
For a thirsty flintrock flaming hangover.
I never paid them any serious mind;
You know how it is, there's a kind
Of crazy gets in the blood and nothing but
The worst that can happen will ever get it out.
The worst that can happen never happened to me,
But there was something that came mighty nigh.

This frolic girl that lived up Smathers Hill—
I won't say her name, because she still
Lives there—appeared to be the country sort
Of willing gal you always hear about
And generally never meet. But we'd fall in

Together now and then, and now and then
She'd take a snort if it was offered nice.
And so we horsed around, more or less
Like kids, had us a drink or two and a laugh.
I'd make a pass, and she was hanging tough.
But finally we found ourselves in bed
Together, and I don't think that that's so bad
And awful Jesus will lock the door on you.
Nothing but an itch for something new
And curious, nothing but a sport we giggled
Over when I laid hold of something that jiggled.
Where by God's the harm? You got a friend
Who right-now needs some help, you lend a hand,
Don't you? And never think about it after.
Well, if a woman's lost the man who loved her
And is feeling low, why not pitch in
And give? Every preacher's brimstone bitching
Won't turn my mind on that. —But looky-here,
I might be trying to make myself seem square
And open. To tell the truth, we sneaked around.
That's what was so unpeaceable in my mind. —
We sneaked and thought we were secret as mice;
But Pigeon Forks is a mighty little place,
And two Saturdays hadn't passed before
Elsie found out what we were doing, and more,
A whole lot more, besides. You'd think the tale
Would talk about our diddling, but that wasn't all
By any means. These snuffbrush gossips hear
A story, they fix it up till it's as queer
And messy as the wiring in radios
And sinful as Nevada. Say adios
To anything you know's the truth when those
Old ladies start to twist it by the nose.

But she got enough of the truth to smell
Us out. And planned with that durn preacher they'd tail
Us around until they saw the living sight

Of us having some fun while they were not.
I'll make it short. They caught us plain as day
Light in her bedroom. Before you could say
Jack Robinson they flung the door wide open
And there we were. Halfway between hoping,
Wishing, farting and fainting, I leapt out
The window and ran like a rabbit showing my scut,
Scared enough to run to Cherokee,
And praying that the shooting wouldn't hit me.
Feet don't fail me now. But it wasn't feet
That done me in. The wind lifted a sheet,
A great big white bedsheet, on the backyard
Clothesline into my eyes. I went down hard.
The clothesline caught me under the chin and down
I went, out cold and nekkid on the ground.

From here on in it's awful mortifying
To talk about. In fact, I'd still be lying
If Elsie was still alive to hear . . . When I
Woke up all I could see was a kind of sky,
A wet-white sky that covered me from head
To toe. It came to me that I was dead—
She'd shot my vitals out—and here's the shroud
They buried me in like a cold and clammy cloud.
I fought against it like an animal,
Kicking and clawing, and got nowheres at all.
I hollered till I damn near deefed myself
And thought how I'd do it all different if
I could only live my earthly life again:
I'd be a sweet and silent religious man.

What had happened was, they'd sewed me in,
In one of those wet bedsheets off the line,
Elsie and the preacher. What they'd done
I didn't know then. But that was *their* good fun.

Then: *pow*! Pow pow pow. I took
Some knocks so hard my suffering eyeballs shook.

Pow pow pow. *So this is hell,*
I thought, *and I've deserved it about as well*
As anybody ever. But still it seemed
Unfair, and came on quicker than I'd dreamed.
You think a sinner would get some reprieve,
If only lying a half-hour in his grave.
But no. Immediately they'd hauled me down
And made a marching drum out of my skin.
I was squealing like a little piggy, not
So much from pain as out of fear of what
Was coming next. I dreaded the boiling oil
And the forty hotted pitchforks up my tail.
Go on and laugh, but I am here to tell
You that if there really is a Hell,
Elsie helped plan it. —Because it wasn't God,
But Elsie laying on with a curtain rod.

There's not much left to say. Finally
Her strength gave out, and there she let me lie,
And went off home. And after the awfullest struggle
I got myself unwrapped and crawled, like a bug will
Crawl, out of that wet sheet. There wasn't a scrap
To wear. I went home dressed like a drowned Arab.

I was a sobered feller. Every time
I'd think of another woman there'd come a flame
Rash all over my skin and I'd remember
Having my ass dressed out like sawmill timber.
And the sight of a hanging bedsheet has reminded
Me, and my dick shrunk up till a flea couldn't find it.

"Virgil, your Elsie did you a sight of good,
Made you respectable," my father said.
"Too bad I can't drink with a man on Reform."

"A drink, you say?" he said. "Well, where's the harm?"

IX Remembering Wind Mountain at Sunset

Off Hurricane Creek where
the heady rattlers even the loggers
abash, out of Sandy
Mush and Big Laurel and
Greasy Branch, off the hacksaw edge of Freeze Land,
those winds huddle in the notch
atop Wind Mountain, where counties Madison
and Buncombe meet but never join.
Hardscrabble Aeolus,
that stir of zephyrs is the sigh of poor
folk screwed in between the rocks up
Meadow Fork and Sugar Camp and Trust, Luck,
Sliding Knob, and Bluff.
A lean wind and a meat-snatcher. Wind
full of hopeless bones.

High on Wind Mountain I heard
from the valley below
the wearied-to-silence lamentation of busted hands,
busted spines, galled mules and horses, last breeze
rubbing the raw board-edge of the corncrib,
whimper of cold green beans in a cube of fat,
the breathing of clay-colored feet unhooked
from iron brogans.
A glinty small miasma
rises off the rocks in the cornfield.
The cowbell dwindles
toward dusk.

I went walking up Chunky Gal
To watch the blackbird whup the owl.

Friend, you who sit where some money is,
I tell you, Sometimes the poor are

poor in spirit, the wind is robbing
them of breath
of life, wind from always Somewhere Else,
directionless unfocused desire,
but driving the young ones like thistle seed
toward Pontiac, Detroit, Cincinnati,
Somewhere, wherever is money,
out of the hills.
Can't make a go
in bloody Madison, too much the rocks
and thickety briars suck the breath of the hand.
Suck the womenfolk to twig-and-twine
limberjacks, suck the puckered houses sad,
tumbly shack by blackberry wilderness
fills to the ridgepole with copperhead
and sawbriar. The abandoned smokehouse
droops, springhouse hoards dead leaves.

I see blackbird fighting the crow
But I know something he don't know.

Over Hunger Cove
the rain-crow keeps conjuring rain
till Shitbritches Creek is flooded, tobacco
drowned this year one more year,
the township of Marshall bets half its poke
and the French Broad takes it
with a murmur of thunder.
Lord, let these sawtooth tops
let me breathe, give me one good stand
of anything but elderbush and milkweed,
I'll keep Mama's Bible dusted off,
I'll try not to murder
for spite nor even for money,
just let that wind hush
its bones a little and not fly so hard
at the barn roof and the
halfbuilt haystack, I'll go to the Singing

on the Mountain with Luramae this
time I swear I will.

Fished up Bear Creek till I was half dead.
Caught a pound of weeds and a hornyhead.

Where you're from's
Hanging Dog, ain't it, boy I knowed
your daddy years back, that was your Uncle
Lige wasn't it lost his arm at
the old Caldwell sawmill, they called him Sawmill
after, took to hunting sang
and medicine root, heard old Lige had died,
is that the truth, I disremember, he
was how old? Hundred and forty-nine
counting nights and hard knocks,
that's what he told me, I'll never forget.
Standing right there by that stove he said it.

If you could eat the wind,
if you could chew it and swallow
it for strength like a windmill.
If anything could be made of this wind in
winter with its scythes of ice when it comes dragging
blue snow over the ridgetops and down
the mountainsides here to the house, finds any
little cranny, wind squirms through the holes
like an army of squirrels.
Go over and sit by the fire, won't
be long till your fingers turn blue again
anyhow. Somehow
I don't have my proper strength
a-winters, been to the doc how many times,
it's a poser to him says he, I told him
Doc I just get down weak as rag soup and
he says, Maybe you need a rest, By God
rest I says, reckon maybe I do,
why don't I lay up here for a while.

I saw blackbird fighting the hawk,
He whupped his hiney with a pokeweed stalk.

And then he says, Now how you
going to pay me? I says, Pay you doc, you'll just
have to garnisheer them Rest Wages.

Two women fighting over a box of snuff,
Lost three tits before they had enough.

First snow like a sulphate powder, bluish,
and up-top the trees like frozen lace, crystal white
against the crystal blue of morning north,
look fragile as tinsel, no wind yet much,
only down the back of your neck now and again to
remind you how long about milking
time it'll come on.
It'll come, everything hurtful will come on.
Here is the place where pain is born.
No salve or balm.
Ever you notice how deep cold the rocks get?
No I mean it, you hoeing round in the field
summertime, hit rocks, sparks
jumping every whichway, come winter
you can beat all day on a rock with a crowbar,
never see spark one, rocks
get froze up deep in the heart is why, told
my oldest boy, No wonder our raggedy
ass is cold, even the goddam rocks
have done give up.

            And if you was to get
a little warm, go in by the cookstove there,
just makes it worse, wind when
you go out peels the feeling-warm right
off, you'll think you've fell
in Spring Creek River, way it goes over you
ice water, but the funny part is, come summer

same wind out of the same place,
feels like it's pouring out of a coalstove,
ain't a breath of soothe in it. Now that's funny.

Maybe the wind like that gets me so low.
Hateful to think of it stepping on my grave
when I'm took off, and then still clawing
you know the apple tree
and the hayfield and the roof of this house,
still clawing
at my young ones after I'm laid safe
out of it. What's the relief in that?
Under the sod you know here'll
come that Freeze Land wind crawling my joints.

Turkey buzzard took old blackbird flying
Like a pissant riding on a dandelion.

Youngish preacherman, heard him
say they ain't no bad without some good
in it somewhere, wanted
to ask him, What's the good in poison oak,
tell me because I can raise twenty solid acres
right in a jiffy, sawbriar too, didn't think
what was the good of this Freeze Land wind, you
know it gets so much inside you, never think
about it being anything, I mean
nothing, just there is all, not anything.
Something you can't see like that you never think.
Like that War in Europe, what'd I know
back here in the stump roots, but they stuck
me over there in the mud
till wild rose and ragweed took my bottom land.

For fighting niggers and hauling loads,
Pulled fifteen months on the county roads.

Friend, you who sit
in the vale of comfort,

consider if you will that there are corners
in this flab land where shale edge
of hunger is chipping out
hearts for weapons, man don't
look from year to year but day by day
alone, suffering of flesh
is whetting the knife edge of spirit in
lower Appalachia, margins
where no one thinks you're his buddy,
don't come driving that big-ass Lincoln
up Hogback Ridge if you like your paint job,
they's some old
bushy boys in here kill a man for
a quarter, eyegod, you seen about that feller
in the papers? I'm not saying
what I've heard about them Henson brothers,
you knowed old man Henson or your daddy did,
him that burned the sheriff
out, had two boys nigh
as lowdown as ever he was, I
don't know what-all I've heard tell.

Up on Wind Mountain there ain't no help.
Blackbird went and killed hisself.

Friend, sit tight on your money,
what you've got, there's a man
on a mountain thinks he needs it worse.

All this I heard in the stir
of wind-quarrel in Wind Mountain notch,
rich tatters of speech
of poor folk drifting like bright Monarchs.
And then on the breeze a cowbell,
and the kitchen lights went on in the valley below,
and a lonesome churchbell
calling
home, home, home, home

till I could bear it no more.
Turned my back.
Walked down the mountain's other side.

They hauled old blackbird's carcass away,
Buried him head-down-deep in red clay.

Here comes the preacher to say the last word:
"It's a fitten end for old blackbird."

X Hallowind

Setting: Halloween, 1961; Durham, N.C.
Personae: Reynolds Price, Susan, Fred, the rain, the wind

        Fred
Listen to it skirl the roof
And tear the ragged eaves as if
The world outside weren't room enough!

        Reynolds
Voices.

        Fred
    What do they say?

        Reynolds
            "In, in."
The ghosts of stories not yet written
Lisp and whimper like dead men.
It's up to us to chronicle
Their thoughts, that death not treat them all
The way that life did, flat forgetful.

        Fred
What a swarm of stories there
Must be, to overload the air
With voices as loud as a river's roar.

        Reynolds
The number, of course, is infinite.

        Fred
Why couldn't a single story tell it
All?

        Reynolds
    Ah, that's the helpless poet
In you, the need to generalize
From yours to all men's destinies.

For fiction, those are pompous lies
Which try to stretch the single stories
Into laws akin to physical laws.

Fred
You're no one to talk. *A Long
And Happy Life* will make as strong
An example as any poet's song.
What is it but the ancient tale
Of Cupid and muddled Psyche? All
That's added is the motorcycle.

Reynolds
That's not the way I see it. These
Are Warren County sweethearts whose
Lives shape local clarities.

Fred
Suppose, though, that I choose to read
The myth within it. Is it so bad
To add more meaning to each word?

Reynolds
But do you add or take away?
A certain lake, a certain tree,
A particular girl on a certain day—
A fleeting tang in Carolina . . .
You'd give that up for some diviner
Heavy symbol?

Fred
                    But if I find a
Paradigm as old as fiction
Itself conformably mixed in?

Reynolds
Well, that requires some hard reflection.
If you think it's there it's there,
I guess. It could be anywhere,

Or not at all. *Things as they are*:
That's the novelist's true belief.
I regard the "symbol" as a thief
Which steals the best parts of a life.

Fred

I think I don't believe you quite.

Reynolds

I'm overstating it a bit
To make my point. Jim Applewhite
Would have conniptions if he were here—

Fred

And Spender too.

Reynolds
—*Things as they are*:
I'll stand by what I see and hear.

Fred

And does that mean the poet's blind
And deaf? Let's say he's trained his mind
To hear all, multivoiced as wind.

Reynolds

Wind's what the poet cannot fix;
The current of life from Eden to Styx
Demands an accounting of *the facts*.
Poems are maimed by their timelessness,
Lack of distinction in *was* and *is*,
That stony stillness like a star of ice.
The *symbol* is at last inhuman,
A cruel geometry, and no man
Ever loved one like a woman
Or a novel.

Fred
Oh, come now. Yeats—

Reynolds
I except of course the crazy poets
Who can fall in love with rocks and he-goats.

(*Enter Susan with tea and cakes.*)

Fred
Now just a minute—

Susan
                    Boys, boys.
I'm surprised you make such a dreadful noise.
—Reynolds, your Oxonian poise!
Old Fred *never* had a grain
Of couth, but you're a *gentleman* . . .
Don't you-all hear how the wind's brought rain?

(*They fall silent and listen. Susan pours.*)

Fred
The most symbolic line there is,
And fullest of hard realities,
Is Shakespearean: "Exeunt omnes."

Reynolds
Your poet's a foe to love and laughter.
Here's the line one gives one's life for:
"They all lived happily ever after."

Susan
I wish I weren't a writer's wife.
I'd live as harmless as a leaf
And cuddle up in a dear warm life.

                    The Rain (to The Wind)
What say we work us up some brio
And drown this silly wayward trio?
My favorite line is "Ex Nihilo."

The Wind

Leave them in peace, if peace there is
For their clamorous little species;
Let them relish their flimsy wishes.
Tomorrow and tomorrow we
Advance against them frightfully.
This night at least they have their say
Together; and the force of Time
Upon their arts, upon slant rhyme
And paragraph, delays for them.
It's soon enough that we dissolve
Their names to dust, unmoving move
Against their animal powers to love
And weep and fear. It's all too soon
They grow as silent as the moon
And lie in earth as naked bone.
We'll let them sit and sip their tea
Till midnight; then I'll shake the tree
Outside their window, and drive the sea
Upon the land, the mountain toward the Pole,
The desert upon the glacier. And all
They ever knew or hoped will fall
To ash . . . Till then, though, let them speak
And lighten the long dim heartache,
And trifle, for sweet trifling's sake.

XI   Wind Subsides on the Earth River

Every water is asleep.

The wind only
Gentles the earth to breathing, to body of breath, it is
This wind from the tips of mountains and from hollers,
Saying, *Home, home,*
Earth is home. Where have we not drifted in fire,
In water, in air?
                    But Earth is the mouths of wind.

My sister wind, wind my mother,
You my confusion of fingers,
I know I shift this world an injured air,
I know how I am guilty in too much space,
And how the churchbell lifts its somber redundance.
The churchbell says:
Home, home   home to the animals,
                    home to the crouchings and lickings, home
                    to twilight, to the small coals of old fire.

Susan, have I not loved you?
This world is wind, and homeless.
Here now I lay my stone of fire, crying,
Touch me, touch, I cannot come apart from the wind.

I come apart from the wind, crying,
Touch me, bright river, your sleeping
Makes this earth domestic.

                    Wind, it is the last thing
On Earth, kissing the petrified rubble of dream.
I dream, Susan, we are not wind;
I dream we are the breath and flame of the last fire that lived.
Earth huddles to our hands,

                    hands coming apart now
To water, hands luckless in earth, this earth
With its mouths of wind coming apart to mind,
Mind drifting to fire, to water, no bodies,
What can we love with?
We cannot love with wind, tell me, Estuary,
We are but both and each.

The wind in the meat night says,
You have no hands, no bodies, you cannot speak.
Our figures
Collide touchless as reflections of Buicks in supermarket windows.
Ghost and no ghost,
I lift you toward that profound atom,
Earth,
I know you dream of.

We have lived to die.
We have lived at last to kiss
Our forefathers
With our green earthlips.

                    Wind

Wind wind
Says, We shall ever.

It does not end like this, wind taking
The last fever of water.
There is a final shore.
In the winds of rocks my blood shall learn to dance.

Susan Susan   this broken tide

Earthsleep

*Now comes the peal of the distant clock, with fainter
and fainter strokes as you plunge farther into the wilder-
ness of sleep. It is the knell of a temporary death. Your
spirit has departed, and strays, like a free citizen,
among the people of a shadowy world, beholding strange
sights, yet without wonder or dismay. So calm, per-
haps, will be the final change; so undisturbed, as if
among familiar things the entrance of the soul to its
Eternal home!*

—Hawthorne

I   Earth Emergent Drifts the Fire River

Shoves us landward, straining and warping like kites.

Yellow ring of earth bobs up to eye-level
At the blowing window.
                          The cool deep morning
Begins to fashion the trees, flesh-tree
And tree of spirit, haranguing the land with birds.

                          Sleep, love, keep
Still.
Why would you ever wake?
My mind in your blood discovers each dream of earth
And every earth. Mind coming apart to blood, windblown
Islands of fire voyage that headlong ocean your blood,
Blood's-breath warms and swells the bedroom,
Room where sleep takes its monstrous earthshape, room where
My thirty-fifth birthday, 28 May 1971, waits
To devour my bit of flesh,
My bit of fire.

Terrible to know this day raising over houses its wind,
Wind of change no real change,
Fire colors the military maps, each village a red coal,
Water leached through sand leaves
Not the vaguest map-shape, history
Too thirsty, bloodthirsty; and earth
Adrift in wind.
The birdsong tiers of my dream are the screams
Of the immolated and the self-immolated.
And the drowned men swim unbearably toward us.

                          The window is raucous with sunlight,
Water-warble, daybreeze, the window
Opens into the furnace of spirit, the cranky

Obbligato of bluejay, stinksparrow, opens the flames of morning.
The cool contralto mourning dove
Is the one clear note of soothe in the world
Going up in flame. *The furious net*
Of daylight plumbs the bed. We are, Susan, lifted
Dripping with sparkle toward the earliest sun.
In dayfire the trees lose their forms, green leaves
Glow like knifeblades, the waters down
Among the dead rob the birds of song, light
Strips world-shape to half-dream, it is the
Windy delirium of fire, the Silver Planet is taking our
World of warm wet, I do not wish to be
Consumed by spirit merely, I do not wish
To be consumed. I do not
Wish to be. I do
Not wish.

               An ecstasy of forgetting
And aspiring. What there is in emptiness,
What limits, what foreknowledge, what improbable coldness, what
Hatred for the spirit-tree, the tree of flesh,
What there is, let it consume itself,
Let it mass and flounder yonder from the skin
Of things, let it not come nigh this hearth, this hold,
This house, let the cloud of unbeing never touch
Our garish boxes of fervor. Susan, we must dream
The sinewy dream, the dream militant,
We must thrust at bay all that is dreamless.
Here are we perched unsteady on the margin of dream,
Receiving from two worlds their gaudy intelligence.
World of half-sleep,
World of waking,
               where the four-square crucis of elements
Cuts clean across. Yet are we
Given to know beyond these Another,
                     where no water sings with
Its breath of fire, where sunlight the cloud never

Ripens to peach, where the single atoms stray
Lost and touchless, where even the longdrawn shriek
Of history sounds a thin sigh merely, it is
That world we send our fireships to destroy.
Not death, no, there is no
Death, only a deeper dreaming. But there is
                    Nothing,
The black egg seedless hatching its harsh wings.
Yet is Whitman not delivered to it, nor Thoreau.
Nor the human deaths of lovers,
It cannot gorge them.

                    I push more fiercely
My face to your breast, my forehead suckles your shoulder.
Do I not hear in you patches of light
Like the little gold-red marigolds chirping at sunset?
Peeling of sun-skin like the handshaped poplar leaves
Spinning down in first October? Gleams of coins
Of watershine in the white slant dawn?
I hear clearly this jazz of piecemeal light,
Glitter on glitter of melodic line
Atop its dense profound harmony of shadow.
                                    Rattle and thump,
The drumming of sun on the river, what fun,
And that trumpet passage where sunstreak
Goes from treecrown to treecrown like a card trick,
That's the streaming, sun/slice   light/dark   sun/slice,
Of light through the boarded barn. Light is sound,
We hear it in the trees at daybreak.

Falling towers of lace
And spittle:
                    the light in the trees
At daybreak, filigree of sugar icing, it is
A wedding cake, no, it is a highly fanciful birthday cake,
Hullo ole Fred Welcome to Life and Death,
1st day my 35th year the world.
Sun/slice   off/on   dark/light   death/life   dark/light.

                              These waters crept to me
Within the music: sand-thrilled spring water,
The tepid slackwater of West Fork Pigeon River,
Baptismal water, perfume of tongue-and-groove pine,
Steaming lakewater at daybreak. I stroke
The water upward, waking, I
Am rising, I dream no more drowning,
I leap toward the surface, bubbles of breath
Surround my eyes, little worlds in water, spheres
Of perfect music, I shall escape from drowning
Into a world of waters, my grandmother's feet in water
The dreambloated roots of cypress,
Death-well where noon sun is caught,
Water that bears away the whiskey earth, I
Am dreaming these no more, I am content,
Susan, to see you step forward from the drizzle,
Ideal taking form in history, touchpoint of
Vision and blood, your pinkened foot on cool tile,
Here is your towel, rough terry cleanses the
Word of life, you are the spirit of water
By sweet fire tempered to earth, speak you,
Tell me some elder annunciation, tell me
History is being reborn in water, in healing water
Rise all the cities gone down, the nations who
Died in the fire of blood take clean new bodies,
A silver ivy of water reclaims the broken walls,
Unguessed Atlantises poke their streaming heads
Out of the history books, sins of the fathers
To lordly earth overgiven rise
Again now transformed to the great names we feed upon,
The fertile waters of deathsleep manure the flames.

                         "What now can be said of air?"
The small breathing of earth, souls aswoon in wind,
Wind is the suffering of spirit, unfocused
Directionless desire, here driven and there in space
We are unhoused, unhouseled,

Wind Mountain pours its cold poverty on the land,
Searches the man rock-wedged, searches his flesh
Every vulnerable nook of it, his soul
Tatters in barren rocktooth wind,
He dies except he lives, lives exalted
As the burly Spirit uplifts his spirit amid
What poor stones, I go to the mountain
To be upraised humble, on the mountain we spread our
Picnic blanket, my grandfather's evanished church sighs
In the wind, this is the melancholy of never forgetting,
The bones in air, music music of
Expectant freedom, I do desire you now.

Susan, we are gone we have come
To earth.
The resplendent house of spirit bursts around the body.
Mind rises from the ravages of sense
And clothes in dream. Mind, old Crusoe,
Are you here lost with me on this island of fire,
This bright and lonely spark struck off
In the heave of bloodsea?
Earth, where do you take us, will you
Shed us upon the black waters streaming
Deathward?
Will you deliver us to wind,
In wind to suffer shorn of flesh, crying
Our mewling cry?
Or thrust us
Into the fire, into the raging ecstasy
Of purified spirit, of burning foreknowledge?
                                        Do not us Earth
Remember.
            Leave us, mud jumble of mirk
And humus, tucked in the rock heart
Of the mountain, in these stones are seeds of fire,
Dream-seeds which taking root shall renew the world,
Tree of Spirit lifting from the mountain of earth

As the curtains of fire rise behind our eyelids,
Spirit Tree of Fire overglowing all the world,
Seeking with its flower-light
Each crinkle in the rock, each crease
In the dark heart hid from the head.

I feel your touch, Earthflesh,
Here my birthday is.

Birthday 35, 28 May 1971.

Okay,
I gird myself.
I'll wear my clothes, my naked clothes.

> *Rock me gently, gentle Earth,*
> *In air, in fire, in water, I am steeped.*
> *And every promise I shall keep*
> *That I have promised while I slept.*

Hello Destiny, I'm harmless Fred,
Treat me sweet Please.

II   My Mother's Hard Row to Hoe

Hard, I say. Mostly I can't think how
To make it clear, the times have changed so much.
Maybe it's not possible to know
Now how we lived back then, it was such
A different life.
                    "Did you like it?"
                                        I

Felt that I had to get away or die
Trying. I felt it wasn't *me* from dawn
To dawn, "slaving my fingers to the bone,"
As Mother used to say; and yet so bored
It was a numbing torture to carry on.
Because that world was just plain hard.

Mother was always up at five o'clock,
Winter and summer, and jarred us out of bed
With her clanging milkcans and the knock
Of water in the pipes. Out to the shed
I went, and milked five cows and poured the milk
Into the cans—so rich it looked like silk

And smelled like fresh-cut grass. Then after that
The proper work-day started. I did what
She told me to, no never-mind how tired
I was, and never once did she run out,
Because that world was just plain hard.

Because from May through August we put up hay
And worked tobacco and, sure as you were born,
We'd find the hottest stillest July day
To start off in the bottom hoeing corn.
From the pear orchard to the creek's big bend,
Corn rows so long you couldn't see the end;

And never a breeze sprang up, never a breath
Of fresh, but all as still and close as death.
We hoed till dark. I was hoeing toward
A plan that would preserve my mental health,
Because that world was so almighty hard.

I'd get myself more schooling, and I'd quit
These fields forever where the hoe clanged stone
Wherever you struck, and the smell of chickenshit
Stayed always with you just like it was your own.
I felt I wasn't *me*, but some hired hand
Who was being underpaid to work the land,
Or maybe just a fancy farm machine
That had no soul and barely a jot of brain
And no more feelings than any cat in the yard
And not good sense to come out of the rain.
That world, I say, was just too grinding hard.

But I'd learn Latin and Spanish and French and math
And English literature. Geography.
I wouldn't care if I learned myself to death
At the University in Tennessee
So long as I could tell those fields goodbye
Forever, for good and all and finally.
—"You really hated it then?"
                                        No, that's not true.
. . . Well, maybe I did. It's hard to know
Just how you feel about a place; a blurred
Mist-memory comes over it all blue,
No matter if that place was flintrock hard.

There were some things I liked, of course there were:
I walked out in the morning with the air
All sweet and clean and promiseful and heard
A mourning dove—. . . *No! I couldn't care.*
You've got to understand how it was *hard*.

III   My Father Washes His Hands

I pumped the iron handle and watched the water
Cough his knuckles clean. Still he kept rubbing,
Left hand in his right like hefting a baseball;
The freckles might have scaled off with the clay.
But didn't. They too were clay, he said, that mud
The best part maybe of apparent spirit.

"What spirit?" I asked.
                        He grinned and got the soap
Again and sloshed. A bubble moment I saw
Our two faces little in his palm.
"The Spirit of Farming," he said, "or the Soul of Damnfool."
Our faces went away and showed his lifeline.
"Damnfool why?"
                        "A man's a fool in this age
Of money to turn the soil. Never a dime
To call his own, and wearing himself away
Like a kid's pencil eraser on a math lesson.
I've got a mind to quit these fields and sell
Cheap furniture to poor folks. I've got a mind
Not to die in the traces like poor Honey."
(Our jenny mule had died two weeks before.)
"A man's not the same as a mule," I said.

He said, "You're right. A man doesn't have the heart . . .
We buried Honey, me and Uncle Joe,
While you were away at school. I didn't tell you.
Two feet down we hit pipe clay as blue
And sticky as Buick paint. Octopus-rassling,
Uncle Joe called it. Spade would go down
Maybe two inches with my whole weight behind
And come up empty. Blue glue with a spoon.
I soon decided to scale down the grave.

I told him straight, *I'm going to bust her legs*
And fold them under. His face flashed red at once.
My God, J.T., poor Honey that's worked these fields
For thirteen years, you'd bust her legs? I nodded.
She can't feel a thing, I said. He says,
By God I do. I told him to stand behind
The truck and stop his ears. I busted her legs.
I busted her legs with the mattock, her eyes all open
And watching me crack her bones and bulging out
Farther slightly with every blow. These fields
Were in her eyes, and a picture of me against
The sky blood-raw savage with my mattock.
I leaned and thumbed her eye shut and it was like
Closing a book on an unsatisfactory
Last chapter not pathetic and not tragic,
But angrifying mortifying sad.
The harder down I dug the bluer I got,
And empty as my shovel. It's not in me
To blubber, don't have Uncle Joe's boatload
Of whiskey in my blood yet. Heavy is how
I felt, empty-heavy and blue as poison.
So maybe it's time to quit. The green poison
Of money has leached into the ground
And turned it blue. . . That grave is mighty shallow
That I dug, but I felt so out of heart I couldn't
Make myself go farther and farther down.
I stopped waist-high and we built up a mound
That will soak away by springtime and be level."

"Are you really going to quit the farm?" I asked.
"I wouldn't quit if I could get ahead,
But busting my behind to stay behind
Has got to be the foolishest treadmill a man
Could worsen on. The farm can wait; there's money
To be made these days, and why not me?
Better me than some cheap crooks I know of,
And that's a fact."

"Whatever you say," I said,
"It's kind of sad, though. . . And now old Honey's gone."
"*Gone?* Six nights in a row I'd close my eyes
And see her pawing up on her broken legs
Out of that blue mud, her suffering hindquarters
Still swallowed in, and in her eyes the picture
Of me coming toward her with my mattock;
And talking in a woman's pitiful voice:
Don't do it, J.T., you're breaking promises. . . .
And wake up in a sweat. Honey's not gone,
She's in my head for good and all and ever."
"Even if you quit the farm?"
                              "Even if."

I handed him the towel. He'd washed his hands
For maybe seven minutes by the clock,
But when he gave it back there was his handprint,
Earth-colored, indelible, on the linen.

IV   The Peaceable Kingdom of Emerald Windows

Chortlings of the green uproar of Earth,
Tree-dream, weed-dream, the man within the tree,
Woman within the weed, babies inhabit
Tea roses, at the bottom of the trumpet
Of day lily lies the yellow tabby cat,
Blackberry vine a whirlpool of green blaze,
And kudzu the Great Wall of China, oppossum
Of apple, plum tree is a sea urchin here
By the bridge of hills, crown of whitethorn bleeds
The broken sigh of hills, the hills launch here
Windows windows, summer dream is a freshet
Of windows, raindrop how much window, raindrop
An eye of glass, it is a window of
Deep sadness, it is the lover's tear of goodbye,
Goodbye I perceive to be a human creature.

Goodbye the waters of air are frisky strings.

Goodbye it is the fleeting of gorged bees.

Farewell, la Terre est veuve, farewell, goodbye.

Cheerful sixty-year-old smiling ladies,
If you could know how you sweeten my dream of stone,
You would will me all your gardens green
And send your daughters out to the shouting hayfield
With jugs of chime-clean water. The horses delicious
With sweat sang the old familiar hymns.
Down the alfalfa fell; the crickets rose,
A patent leather cloud of squeaky buttons.
I had not known that bend of river was scythe
To the other shore us gathering.
Mother and father we are distilled, the golden
Sweats of eternity surround us, heat.

The single raindrop gives us light enough
To read whole acres of Debussy, Thoreau.
And the loud hayfield diminishes to a tear,
It is the grandmother's tear of parting. Goodbye.
Amid the riotous Waterloo of hay
I think of a book open in the empty house,
It is a chapter of Psalms, and the table
Is set with tinware, Father may we go in
To dinner, the buttermilk is poured, green beans
Are fast asleep in the lukewarm oven.

O the raindrop's shape, I take its shape
To huddle, hands between my knees, in the form
The doe hare has warmed in the lespedeza,
Sweet placenta-curl, the rain is a squad
Of wet grasshoppers, me and the terrapin, us
Is asshole buddies, gaudier now in water,
What you think, bro? *Move in this wet, you crazy?*

Where rain takes its luckiest shape, the tin roof by
The rusting railroad track, where-O-where's
My tin roof sweetheart, we can get it on
On the sacks of cottonseed meal under the clatter,
No one not even the rain has such big tits,
Lend me your lip a minute, willya, lovechile?
Don't tell me I can't taste in every nook
Of flesh the hayfield wet with terrapins
And the rainsoaked cornbread and crickets and the sun,
The rainsoaked sun settles in the form
In the hay in the world in the green green hand.

The world is before the rain.

Even the downpour, Noah's deluge, is thirsty
For rain as thick as spikes, no rain is manly
Enough, we want rains of sunshot water,
Rains of quartz, rains of clover, rains
Of the blood of the curly lamb with the shepherd's staff,

Rains of semen, rains of eyes, rains
Of windows coming down like guillotines,
Windows windows raining everywhere
Their thrilling clarities of pity. Rains
Of fire.

Reach me my bumbershoot of heady ego,
I'll walk a mile or three with thee, my friend,
We'll go conversing the fields of emerald,
Reminiscing Schopenhauer, or,
If you prefer, Mozart. Pass me a light,
My matches are wet. There's some have told me, Uncle,
This world is not for real, and maybe it's so.
Are your sox as sopping as mine? An Ideal World
They say reposes in Heavenly Peas somewhere
'Midst the *Azur*, a sleepy flea market of Forms,
Kraters, amphorae, tragic destinies,
Ideas, and not a blunder in the whole blame lot.

And maybe it's so, though it sounds like a Grand Hotel
Emptied out because of chicken pox.
The Ideal World must be mighty fine,
Man wouldn't ever have to mow the lawn,
But say, Uncle Body, wouldn't our fingers starve?
Even the women there have got no luscious.

We'll walk and talk and gawk. See the flower,
Uncle, see the stone dissolving to rain
In the rain, observe the oaks. See Spot run.
Hello Dick and Jane, Uncle Body
Says you're dead, lie down with me in the form
The rabbit curled, we'll watch the world go by,
We'll look up the dresses of tan-legged women oh boy
See the mouth in the moss. See Spot run.
World-wound, come and get me, I'm dying for blood.
The goldenrod, shouldering its load of water,
Brighter than the epaulettes of Napoleon's army,
Grows stalwart at the end of sneezy summer;

Fullness of cloud, fullness of hay, erect
Strait barns, tobacco thinking of mellowing,
The hounds begin to itch for the crafty coon.
Hard sour apples are aching for my pocket,
And, Uncle Body, my teeth are longing for bitter.
Let it come down, let it all come down, summer
On its knees, and autumn fulsome as
An opera matron shall take the hill and sit there
Eating bonbons while the crickets warm
Their fiddles. Let it. Let it all go smash.
O what worms we are, ain't it the berries?

In the fields of Elysium, Uncle, we'll meet Gilbert White.
He'll have a smiling preoccupied quizzical phiz
And keep forgetting our names. Merely we want
To hear his mumble: "Woodruff blows. Martins cling
& cluster in a very particular manner.
Cucumbers come. Wheat mends . . ." Stuff like that.
I could listen all day, get drunk as a Hubbard squash.
We'll meet Linnaeus too and André Michaux
And William Bartram, Colette, rare Ben Franklin.
But it's more fun to think whom we *won't* meet.
I've got a little list, as long as the River Nile.
Am I boring you, Uncle Body?
What you want, then? A game of catch? A woman?
A corned beef sandwich obscene with Russian dressing?
All the world is lit for your delight,
Old buddy, hook it to your hulk both hands,
It's a worship of God, though kinda primitive
I admit. But then we-all is a primitive sort
Of animule.

   Help help I'm freezing to death
Here where this blizzard's lying heaped like a
Linen closet. . . Ah no, it's only a field
Of Queen Anne's Lace, no colder than a peach,
The delicate granules troubling my rib, goosing

Behind and afore as I walk snowblind to the fence.
Suppose the world went pure like this all over.
Would I be a better man? No:
Just more conspicuous. Still, in this whited
Sugar-acre I feel purified. . .
Am I an angel already? Let me lift
My wings, let me sing a salving psalm:

"I'm Popeye the sailor man!"

Reckon not. But I'll sing sweeter bye
And bye, we'll all sing like the dead men sing,
Notes as silv'ry sound as soap bubbles
From the pipe drifting out over our blue blue childhood.

I'll say this about the *Book of Earth*,
The guy who wrote it didn't cheat a jot,
Even the footnotes are brimming over with matter,
Matter aye and spirit too, each
And every page is chock to stupefying,
Any page as good as any other.
   . . . Oh sure, Jean-Paul, there's a chapter on "Misery,"
And one on "Disease," a deadly dark one, "Torture,"
But tell you what, I'll trade mine for which
Ever one you choose, I'll still break even.
Bring me your tarred, your poor, your muddled asses,
I'll bear the burden on't. What I care, bo?
It's only the suffering of children that truly hurts,
Most of the others just ain't learned to read good yet.
Lemme check the Index, what'll I find,
Hemorrhoids, aw rite, fetch it hither,
I got a gut of cheerful iron, believe.
Can't be worse than reading William Buckley.

The horses thrust the breath-brown ground behind us.
Why mayn't I ride this rattletooth snagfinger
Chafeballs hayrake from here to Zanzibar?
I'll ride it flat to Heaven who'll say me Nay?

The horses are willing, been a long time ready.
Bay Maude says to Jackson: "Don't let's stop
At windrow-end, good fellow, I feel the edge
Of the world just barely beyond my hooftip,
I'm gonna make the Leap of Faith. Are you
With me?" And sober blaze-faced Jack replies:
"I'm more the pragmatist, my dear, as well
You know. It's you I've ever put my faith in.
If you consider these old bones can do it,
I'll follow you to God's dread-honey heart,
You know I will." And Maude: "I'm deeply touched,
Old lover. Maybe we'd better delay a while?
If you're feeling poorly we ought to wait until
You regain your strength, you'll enjoy it more."
"Alas, my sweet, that might in me you knew
Of old never shall return, I think.
These fields have made of me a plodding old coot;
My mind's about as sprightly as a shelf of Dreiser,
These trembling legs, everyday I curse them."
"Don't talk like that. I wasn't serious, you know.
It was just the sort of silly whim a female
Will now and then get in her head. I didn't
Actually consider going." "But you did, my love,
And now regard for me is all that keeps
You back. Go make your Leap of Faith, the grandest
Thing left in my life for me to see.
I'll urge you on with the cheerfullest hurrah.
I know you can do it." "Lacking you, I can't.
Already I'm tired. Let us just go home now."
I ride the clashbutt hayrake to the barn,
Which is heaven. Barn is home. Home is heaven.
The barn resounding like a churchbell in
The rain, *home, home, home.*

       Upshoot of crickets, butterflies, dust
       And grasshoppers precedes the tearing mower
       In the field everywhere, the visible

Ascension of a strain of Beethoven,
The hayfield birthing music, music,
A harmony of heat-breath, dark-powered
Green juices of the stalks, the blood
Of snakes and baby rabbits the mower spits
Up and out, a portable fountain
Of dear death-life, a man could
Lose a finger and a foot, lose
All thinking to watch the stalks fall neat
Like tumblers toppling off a shelf . . .
The Little Ones have lost their sky.

Our sky bulging like a sack of anthracite flowers,
Rain soon, pile that alfalfa in, rain-rot
Will heat it and eat it, keep it moving, boy,
Keep that pitchfork puffing, don't let me catch you
Heaving a pauseful sigh, we got to pitch
And poot, I'll tell you a secret, I got a bottle
Of Virgil Campbell's applejack hid behind
A joist in the hayloft, we get this in
Before the sky busts loose we'll have us a sup,
Ho there Jackson whoa-haw boy back up
Aw rite getter goin at's aw rite now whoa.

"Jack, my love, have you ever heard such idiot
Instructions in all your life?" "Never have I,
Dear Maude, these fools are half-hysterical.
Why should anyone so fear a little water?"

That blue valley between the thunderheads
Expands, contracts, like an accordion.
Our valley between the hills here flexes also
Itself like a handsome woman readying to bathe.
Ain't a blade or twig don't have its tongue out
To taste the promiseful wealthy coolskin downpour.
I'd make a Renaissance poet's wish, to be
The cloud that sluices these hills, fingering fold
And nipple, glacis and flank, cheek and crevice.

162

O sweet mama, I'm dying for you in gallons,
How would I ever stop, once started to come
Down? I'll rain *home* all over us.

My grandmother plants her final fork at the top.
They fling her a rope, she slides off nifty as
A schoolgirl flush with mischief. Surveys the wagon,
Satisfied? Sated, anyhow.
"Take her in, boys, I believe we'll beat the rain."
That's what we do all day, we beat the rain.

V   Susan's Morning Dream of Her Garden

The way a tree climbs down into the earth,
and earth to keep it from drifting like a bed
seizes the cloudmass roots;

and into ground lean the lonely
and elaborate dead as soft as sleet,
burbling one to another always,

a full Four Hundred of juicy talkers; the way
the headstrong sunflower, and boxwood, Harpwoof
Spragglewort, moondime and Dusty Miller, the pansies

with their Pekinese faces, and grimbleweed lift
out and up in light their informal forms,
pistil and petal half-shadow;

is the way my hand goes into the dirt.
Or is it flesh I enter?
My own, or lubberhubby's lying this plot with me?

Haho. He. He is loose in sleep
and musical as a horse, goeth as a zinnia
brave to daybreak and casts a watershaped snore.

Why are men so toady, tell me, touching
the moss and root? I'll tend me well my contrary garden.
Now my rows of queenly corn erupt to cadenza;

and the cabbages unfurl
outward and inward like sentences of Proust,
the sweet rose invites her oriental suitors all

iridescent in green and oil, and yonder my neat row
of bones blooms out mouths of marrow,
yet I am not replete or reconciled.

164

Garden, garden, will you not grow for me
a salon full of billets-doux and turtledoves?
Garden, garden, green tureen,

will you not put me forth the olden ladies upsidedown
in their hooped skirts like the bells of lilies,
their clapper legs chiming sentimental songs?

I long to belong to
the chipper elegance, those centuries where
the hand of man has never said an ugly word.

I own an antique plate in which I see
a little garden with a swing, a young girl in
the swing, tra-la, and flush with birds of every hue,

troo-loo.
The swing-girl's face is a mint of pale pink roses.
In the garden I grow I'm the girl in the swing, ting-a-ling.

And I rise and rise in my swing through the globe
of green leaves giddy till I become
a rose-pink butterfly with arms of eyes.

We whirl, my garden and I, until
the minuet boils, the sun
and moon and ground and tree become a waltzing sea,

a jiggy river of green green
green. Hurl-whorl green in which we roll
as down a well of hay.

I sing as high and clear-O as a finch
in a yellow-green willow tree,
transparent and vivid as dragonflies.

I'd be a fool, a woman's a fool, to be drawn back
into the waking world,
all dinky clutter and dirty bathtub.

You don't catch me yet, New Day, I'm snugging

deeper in the larder of dream,
I'm burrowing like a lovely whistlepig

into the green earthflesh of sleep, keep
your tarnished-silver fingers, Sun, off my bright hair,
off my pillow, my mellow wallow.

I'm diving to a door I sense below,
a door as yellow with catlight as an owl's eye,
that opens truly into the garden

on my antique plate and can draw
my waking body in and there no one
can draw me out again. No use, you-all,

I'm gone beyond your smirch, you can't
get in, I'm the slattern in the pattern,
admire, admire!

. . . But sunlight now comes licking at my dream-door,
boohoo. *Day day go away*,
come again some other sleep.

Yet there's no help for it, and up I go
to breast the unendearing morning,
eject, usurpt, and half-awake.

I lie like cool meat on the bed like a
dimestore plate which has no picture on it,
no pattern at all.

VI   At the Grave of Virgil Campbell

EarthMan, what o' the night? What ruinous juices
Are you fermenting here six feet under?
Never, Virgil, tell me I shan't taste them.
I leak my fervent beer on your smooth stone.

Art gone to earth, old fox? And never a dram
Shall draw thee blathering out again to light?
They've washed and laid you in a Christian plot,
Not even the thirsty widows shall claw you up,
I visit you half-smashed, you'll understand,
There's too many ragshank preachers in these hills
And not a man among them. Let's you and me
Get down, O I mean *down*, and tell some lies
To the worms and minerals. I'll tell them how
You murdered the iron bridge, you tell them sly
About Magruder's goat that wrecked the outhouse,
About the coonhound that could measure lumber,
About the flatland tourister catching the bear,
About Bad Egg that ravaged Madison County,
All that stuff . . . DeathAngel in his nightgown
Will set his candle down to listen and giggle,
All the tenants of the afterlife been saying,
"Just wait till ole Virge gets here, he's a *caution*."

I've been fumbling with some epitaphs
In case you want to try them on for size.
HERE LIES VIRGIL CAMPBELL—ONE MORE TIME.
How's that strike you? A little naked maybe.
Something a bit more classical perhaps?
        SISTE, VIATOR.
        VIRGIL CAMPBELL'S QUIET HERE.
        WHO NEVER WAS BEFORE.

Or:

>HERE'S THE FIRST TIME IT WAS SAID
>THAT VIRGIL CAMPBELL WAS GRAVELY LAID.

Or:

>EARTH, RECEIVE
>YOUR PLAYFUL LOVER
>TO HIS ONE SLEEP
>WITH NO HANGOVER.

I've got no business scribbling epitaphs
For wiser sounder men who can't hit back.
It makes me feel right sanctimonious.
So I've written one for me and here it is:

>THIS ONCE AT LEAST EARTH RAISED HER FACE
>TO ME. FOR THIS COLD KISS
>I HAVE DESERTED LOVE AND BLOOD.
>I PRAY YOU, STRANGER, PRAY ME PEACE.

Well yes *of course* it's got more dignity
Than yours, I wrote it, didn't I? . . . Howzat,
Old mole, you think it's junky-portentous?
But Virgil I'm the *poet*, had my name
In the paper once . . . Okay, here's another:

>HERE LIES FRED
>IN HIS MOSS-GROWN MANSE.
>IF HE'S NOT DEAD
>HE'S MISSING A DAMN GOOD CHANCE.

What you mean, it doesn't scan? Who's
The poet here, godammit? I write how I please.
Awright, awright, let me get a beer,
I'll write myself one last epitaph,
Don't hold your breath, though:

>OLD FRED
>HAS HAD
>   IT.

There I'm through, you're through for sure, we're through
The both of us. *Salute*, I lift my Bud
Beneath the coldstone stonegray winter sky,
I drink your health for any good it'll do you,
I hope it does you oodles, it does me fine.

Here in Checkerboard City I think on bones,
The grave-rat whispers his restless runes in my ear,
The Barrow-Dwellers rise and sit on their names,
There's plenty destiny to go around
In here, I'm not worried I'll get my share.
Just look at the gleaming ghosts of them, Uncle Virgil!
Hard to picture Scruggses and Smatherses in
The gross become so lightly tenuous.
Lie down, spirits, you don't frighten me,
You left your shotguns back among the living.
But stay and tell me: the Mountains Outside Time,
Are they rife enough with coon and possum,
Have you hounds to sniff that spirit-spoor,
Do you gather round the hillside fire
And tell the tales and sip eternal moonshine?
I hope so dearly, save me a lie and a drop.
I *know* there's Whiskey-after-Death, elsewise
You wouldn't waste your time there, would you, Virgil?

You who were overmuch of earth now hold
The earth, the land beyond the dirt, unleasable
Acres of absence shining like tablecloths.
There you harvest Sundays, the long yellow
Sunday afternoons of June, you stack them
Glowing in glowing barns, eternity
Lights up like flax, like Christmas, with the hundred
Thousand billion trillion luminant Sundays.
Think of all those Sundays, Virgil, with not
A preacher in view! And the river furtive with trout,
The whistlepigs adrift in the sassafras,
The blotchy terrapins nudge the plantain,

Eternity at last we all go barefoot.
—This bright vision of Afterward contents me
The way a fire will sing a cat to sleep.

Here in the boneyard all the livelong day
What do you *do*? Count the rich men jamming
The needle's eye as you used to tote up Packards
On the Interstate? Count the surrealists
Trying to squeeze to Heaven through the knothole
In Grandpa's wooden leg? No you don't count,
For where you are no number is or was,
I'll bet it drives the misers crazy, I'll bet
They wish they'd never died in the first place.
I think you must spend your days playing checkers
With Moses and Jacob and the rest of the Bible crew.
Watch out King David, he's got some tricky moves,
And I've heard it said that Ananias cheats.
St. John of Patmos, don't challenge him, that guy's
Zonked out on something absolutely *weird*.
Make sure St. Peter crowns your King, of course
He will I never doubted it an instant.

Is death the cool refreshment I think it is?
Better than taking a leak? Than a fresh-cut chaw
Of Black Maria? Vivider than a dipper
Of milk lifted dripping in the springhouse
Where newt and moss cohabit red and green?
It must be so, I think I wouldn't mind
Now and then a fast cold skinnydip
In death, so long as a cramp wouldn't drag me under.
I don't want to leap for keeps, not yet
Anyhow, just want to wash the fever.
Too many drownings I've seen and had already,
There's an army of drownings been marching this earth so long
That every man among us has been stropped thin,
I'm older and newer than New will ever be,

Gimme a break, sweet Gospel, let me grow
Some skin, the sea is tired of plowing me.
The way these trees have stripped their leaves has gotta
Be right, I'll never write another novel
Full of Detail, my bones clothe over with hunger.

After last week's ice storm, Virgil, I walked
The groves in the suburbs. All the chandeliers
That ever were flew there to roost the trees,
Bare limbs decked out gaudy as matadors
Where sunlight tingled the crooked slicks and notches.
And it came to me the dead rise up in light,
We're skeletons of light we are, dimmed down
In the cloudy season of flesh. Bare bone
Bites through at last, the inner gnaws the outer,
The branches clacked like false teeth in an earthquake.
And when the ice dropped off a Tiffany's window
On the root of the tree I thought it was like a duchess
Readying for a shower, for under all
Her diamonds she's still a duchess, ain't she? You bet
Your ass she is, if you had one to bet.
Sooner or later we take St. Francis' Oath
Of Poverty, donate this human fat
To lizards and grasses, come here kitty, here's
Your bowl of Fred-meat, I hope it serves you better
Than ever it served me, I poisoned it
To sleep with alcohol, moral ideals,
And Poetry. The hard lump in your lunch?
Why that's a *bone mot*, pussycat, took me
Thirty-five ballpoint years excresing that knot,
It must mean something. Everything means something
Even if it's Nothing, aw, stand up
Stand up with me, Virgil, we're holy trees,
Our golden boughs ope the Otherworld,
The flaming ice storms of Eternity
Shall give our bones to chatter like pissed-off squirrels,
Here's our chance to trade lies with the saints,

We'll prop our feet on the porchrail of Afterlife
And tell the seraphim about the catfish
That towed our rowboat up the waterfall,
You reckon they'll laugh and slap their thighs, the angels,
And hand around their rainbow jug of whiskey?
Indeed they will, we'll all be singing the hymns,
The good old hymns, sing Bringing in the Sheaves,
Bawl out Shall We Gather at the River?
And the one that goes:

>How teejus and tasteless the yurrs
>Till Jesus-sweet-face I do see

And all the Carter Family songs that seam
The mindstream, Hello Central Give Me Heaven
And There's a Storm Upon the Ocean, and
Jimmy Brown the Newsboy one thousand times.
But now I remember, Virgil, I've heard you sing,
There's many a man has lost his hope of heaven
For lesser crimes. Oh never mind, we'll all
Sing sweeter in the Bye-&-Bye, we'll sing
Like bristly tomcats under the sexual moon.
What good's an afterlife without our singing?
(What's whiskey without the jazz?) Pass me the bottle,
I feel one coming on, mi-mi-mi-mi,
What's this, it's not a hymn it's a drinking song,
Well, sometimes who can tell the difference?

To hell with the ragshank preachers
   Who made it out sinful to think,
And down with the dustdyed teachers
   Whose veins run Bible-black ink,
And Damn every one of those creatures
   Who told us we oughtn't to drink!
If ever they'd taken a sip
   (From me and Chris Sly
   Here's mud in their eye!)
They'd had more brains and less lip.

But here's to the happy old souls
   Who trip about clinking their chains
In time to the music that rolls
   From the locker of Davy Jones,
And here's to the Hand that controls
   Raw-Head-&-Bloody-Bones!
Let's have us a neat little nip
   (For we and the Host
   Forever cry, "Prosit!")
Before we take our last sleep.

Let's put on our nightcaps of moonshine
   And kneel and mumble our prayers,
In Glory we drunkards will soon shine
   Singing our spiritous airs,
And, tipsy as possums by noontime,
   We'll roll down Pisgah like bears!
So pour us a tight little drop
   (And here's to the Splendor
   Of the Holy Bartender!)
And we're ready at last for our nap.

VII   How to Build the Earthly Paradise:
Letter to George Garrett

> Io vidi già nel comminciar del giorno
> la parte oriental tutta rosata
> e l'altro ciel di bel sereno adorno.
>
> —*Purgatorio*, XXX.

Stone,
   quarried
out of the wistful starpaths,
stone first of all deep sunk into
the toiled-up footing, stone from space,
where the walls dig in their roots and bind
force over force in steady fabric
   rising
     up.

Sand
   next, strewn
white and golden on the hewed-out
stone and somewhat muffling its hunger,
the sand inviting as a table-
cloth, "here spread your quaint paradise,
your long pink carnival of sweetmeats,"
   shining
     soft.

Earth,
   acres
of worm-meal earth over sand and stone,
a dirt so rich our warm rude fingers
tingle inside it, rubbing the plasma
ancestral, rye-flour loam which takes

the signature of hoe and plow,
    sleeping
        long.

      Dead
    people
in earthwrack, in the layered gritcake,
let us gently allay them, the dead
are troublous in their cool sleep, they stir
and grumble, blind wall of hands
beneath, blind well-mouths upthrust,
      water-
        speech.

      Then
    water,
waters forcible in dirt
and flesh, their tendons streak the air,
rounded waters widely vying
the built-in skies, waters that mutter
the double names inside the earth,
      sweep clouds
        through.

      Air
    where light
is and where light is not, it holds the
light the way a hand holds water, and
the dark it holds, air alive as
minnows, windheap, the checkered music
light/dark   light/dark, vision stands
      forth in
      air.

      Green
    plants for
the heart's delectation, the rough-red
singing vine glows with fire-oils, the

willful grasses, daisies gleaming like
turnip watches, slime-mold, orchid,
tiger lilies snapping fence links, the
                modest
                        fern.

                The
        sleeping
and unsleeping animals, alert
with breath and licking the unaddled impulse
that sustains the bones, furred shaggy
or smooth in land or ocean, animals
that make their nests in grass, their
                skins are
                        eyes.

                What,
        Giorgio,
have we omitted? *Men and women
and children?* Let's by all means
have them, by the century and the multitude,
we need some middle-muddle here to keep
the sky from being so polar-miserable
                lonesome
                        cold.

                That's
        how I'd
build it, the Earthly Paradise: no
different, how could it be?, from what
it was ever dreamed, harsh floodtide
of feathervein delight each instant at
every hand, the troubador atoms
                dancing
                        full.

                Is
        it true

already, what if it's true already? and
we have but to touch out to see it
among our amidst, how then can we say
ourselves guiltless ever, not partaking,
forswearing the joyous hale, we ought
                    to be
                            shot.

               No
          more, I
never no more will turn my back
upon, cast down my eyes away from,
that spinning spanning spuming spawning
shoal of burnished juices, the seething
homebrew of creation creating, I swear it
                    in my
                          bones.

              New
          now you
see me a new man, unshucked from
my soiled hide, I'm coming belchlike out of
the cave, make way my friends make way,
here gleaming with unspotted dream, here
clamorous with tincture, is yes your
                old friend
                    Fred.

VIII My Grandmother's Dream of Plowing

I never saw him plowing, but Frank was well
And whole and plowing in the field behind
Jackson and Maude whose heads went up and down
Like they agreed on what they were talking over.
There was a light around him, light he was blind
To, light tolling steady like a bell.
The dirt peeled back from the share like meal, brown
Loam all water-smelling. What he'd uncover
With his plowing I felt I already knew:
He'd turn up that bell from the church the Klan
Burned down because of the Negro organist.
The bell they couldn't find had washed in the tide
Of earth and finally had come to rest
In our own bottom land that used to grow
Tobacco . . .
                    I was wrong; for when the sun
Gleamed on something in the furrow-side
I went to look, and it wasn't a bell at all.
It was a big and shining lump of gold.
It was a Mystery gold, and just the tip
Of it stuck out. With my bare hands I brushed
Away the crumbs and dug it out of the soil.
I got on my knees and tried to wrestle it up,
And after a while I did, aching, and rolled
It out and stood looking at it all hushed.
About as big as a twenty-five-pound sack
Of flour. And burning burning like the flame
Of Moses' bush. It lay there in the furrow
Like, like . . . Oh, I can't say what like.
I picked it up and cradled it to my breast,
Thinking how this was a Gold made out of dream

And now we'd never fear about tomorrow
And give our frets and cares a well-earned rest.

"Is that your baby that was never mine?"
Behind me Frank had stopped the plow. His voice
Came up against me like another person,
Like a stranger maybe intending harm.
His voice was dressed in black and laid a curse on
All the fancies I'd thought up for us.
I turned around to tell him Hush, but then
I knew it *was* a baby in my arm,
The strangest baby. As fat and dimpled as
The Baby Jesus in the pictures on
The Upper Room. And this golden child was
Speaking to me, not just baby-talk,
But real words that I ought to understand.
Except I couldn't hear. Bent my head down
But couldn't hear, no more than you hear the dark.
"It's not my baby, and just never you mind,"
I said to Frank. "This baby I've found will bring
Us luck," I said, "because it turned from gold
To flesh. That means—it has to mean—something
To us, something to help us when we're old."
"We're old," Frank said, "we're old already, Anne.
And, see, the baby's changed to something else.
It's turned into an ugly little man."
I looked, and felt the beating of my pulse
Grow harder in my throat, knowing it was true.

I held to me an evil little goblin
With an evil smile. And, must-be, astray in its mind,
The way its eyes were loose, and its head bobbling
Up and down like corn tassel in the wind.
All over I went water then and trembled
Like a flame of fire. I turned my face away
From Frank. I'd never felt so ashen-humbled.

What had I brought upon us? *Oh what, what?*

Something terrible the field had birthed,
And now I'd gathered it up, and who could say
It wouldn't haunt us forever from this day
Onward? I'd never thought such ugly thought
As standing there with what the plow unearthed
And wishing it would go away. Or die.
That's what I wished: *Please die, and let us be.*

Now here's the awfullest part. What I said
To do, it did. It rolled its eyes glass-white
Back in its head, and kicked and shivered like
A new-born calf, and murmured in white froth
A tiny whimper, and opened on its mouth
A glassy bubble and sucked it gagging back
Into its throat, and opened and closed its throat,
And sighed a sigh, and lay in my arms stone dead.

It was my fault. It turned into a stone,
And it was all my fault, wishing that way.
Whatever harm had the little goblin done?
And now I'd killed it. I began to cry,
And cried so hard I felt my eyes dissolve
To dust, to water, fire, and then to smoke.

"And then you woke," I said, "to the world you love."

"And now I know," she said, "I never woke."

IX My Grandfather Dishes the Dirt

Who is walking on my grave?
Is it my Family up there come to bring
Me flowers, come to have

A latter word or two? It must be Spring,
That's when you always come . . .
When every juice is flourishing,

Have you no better chore than standing about my tomb?
Please understand, I *like* it here,
Dreaming in cold earth my freshened dream.

It's true the things I left behind are dear
To me, and maybe in some ways
Now dearer. The turning of the year

Sweetly I remember, and blue May days
Leap out in my grave sleep
Like sun-drunk butterflies.

But mostly now I keep
My thoughts as cool and quiet as the stare
Of glinting spring water in a tin cup.

I wish that I could share
With you—. . . But no, of course I can't . . .
You know already as you require.

The knowing that now I know would daunt
Your spirits,
Sickly them over with the pale cast of want.

Death disinherits
Us of wanting, I find.
Here where it's

Still not Absolute I'm lying blind
To itch and wish
And still am not resigned.

To tell the truth, I'm devilish
Hard put to it to think
Of anything much to say which

Now you'd care to hear. It's dark as ink
Down here, and kind of lonely,
And as mysterious as a wink;

But you don't want to hear all that. Only
Always my thoughts reach out
To silence, to a stonily

Determined silence, broken by a shout
Now and then of starburst,
Or a glittering rout

Of softly spilling dust.
What's that to you,
Still toiling luck and work and lust?

The dead I'm here to say have nothing to say.
Our job is merely to listen and look
From now until the Judgment Day

When we can see once more in the Judgment Book
All that we've seen already, each nook
And cranny of us forever on display.

Let's let each other alone, for Jesus' sake.

X   Stillpoint Hill That Other Shore

This ground, Susan, is full of hands,
hands filled with earth,
voices of the hands of earth,
the finger-tendrils of earthroots
stroke our bones, this is the hill
at midnight,
the moon devours
bones out of the ground, the moon
signs the firmament
in the steady hand
of the faithful dead. We can read
at last the firepoint
constellations all in the deep
where the other earths are swimming.
The stars see us
with new eyes.

Restored to earth, returned
from earth, our hands
and voices interlace
like the fires of double suns.
Do we see each other,
one another in unsteady
starshine?
Do I unsteady not see
you steady?

This hill above our house,
stillpoint before
the turning begins again,
earth solid to the hand,
earth moveless in time,

comprised
of the husk and marrow of
our dead forefathers.
Unmoving in time,
only the dead are incorrupt.

Time I shall not serve thee.
You Earth I have loved most blest.

Our futures in the dirt
speak to us, saying,
The Old Unmoved is a-movering,
have you yet prepared
your spirit for the starry waters?
I have not I am not,
Earth,
prepared, here let me rest
unready, Susan has taken my hand,
we step forward blind
into the blind windcurrent of the soil.
The murders and betrayals,
wounds, firefevers, bloodtwitchings,
the burning suicides, the tortured genitals,
the vacant children,
ruin of seed, mind-ruin, sleep-ruin,
nightmare of the sickened animals,
hold these in peace away from us
for this moment.
We beaten creatures cannot evermore
bear. Too long
we have thrashed in earthfire,
our limbs quiver,
exhaustion of stale guilt.

Susan has taken my hand, I clutch
her voice though it comes fitful
in the starshot earthdark.
Her voice is in surges
the soothing of a thousand waters.

In veins of my sleep
I feel the piling of those waters,
cool mouths mirroring dark sky
where no words shine, where
the Tree of Spirit lifts its roots
among the black stars whirling
collapsed to nervous cinder.
These are the flower-worlds with all
the visionary petals shriveled away.

Please hold my hand, may we
go down now, home?
Where booklight and kitchen light
furrow the silence?
In the dark, two lights,
like two strokes of a churchbell,
home, home.
Can you not hear it tolling,
our toothsome sleep we may at last attain?
It calls to me, calls,
and my whole blood
is avid for that earth,
that sleep.

Sleeping we are harmless at last.
Through silence moves a cloudless peace.

The peace that shall seize us
in sleepgrip,
that peace shall I tell you
be all the black frenzies of our flesh
in one green cuddle,
let us descend to our house
our bed
and invite the mornings,
the infinite anniversary mornings,
which reach out to touch us
with the hands of one another.

XI   Earthsleep

It is the bottomless swoon of never forgetting.

It is the foul well of salvation.

It is the skin of eternity like a coverlet.

It is a tree of fire with tongues of wind.

It is the grandfather lying in earth and the father digging,
The mother aloft in air, the grandmother sighing.

It is the fire that eats the tree of fire.

It is Susan in the hand of sleep a new creature.

I am a new creature born thirty-five years to this earth
Of jarring elements, its fractuous hold
On the man and woman brings
Earth to bloodmouth.
                              Here where I find
I am I founder.
                    Lord Lord
Let this lost dark not.

Who's used?
Who's not scrawled upon
By the wilderness hand of
Earth and fire and water and air?

How simple simple blessèd simple.

It is the fathomless noon that blossoms after midnight,
And daybreak at the margin of the oaks
Begins to sculpt our sleeping bodies
In the wimpled bed.

What shapes may we take now
Where destiny uncurls its roots of fire?

Let it then be flesh that we take on
That I may see you
Cool in time and blonde as this fresh daybreak.

No one no one sleeps apart
Or rises separate
In the burning river of this morning
That earth and wind overtake.

The way the light rubs upon this planet
So do I press to you,

Susan   Susan

The love that moves the sun and other stars
The love that moves itself in light to loving
Flames up like dew

Here in the earliest morning of the world.

Sir Toby. A false conclusion: I hate it as an unfilled can. To be up after midnight and to go to bed then, is early; so that to go to bed after midnight is to go to bed betimes. Does not our life consist of the four elements?

Sir Andrew. Faith, so they say; but I think it rather consists of eating and drinking.

Sir Toby. Thou art a scholar; let us therefore eat and drink. Marian, I say! a stoup of wine!

—*Twelfth Night*